The Two Of Us

Four One-Act Plays

by Michael Frayn

A SAMUEL FRENCH ACTING EDITION

SAMUEL FRENCH

FOUNDED 1830

New York Hollywood London Toronto

SAMUELFRENCH.COM

CONTENTS

THE TWO OF US comprises four one-act comedies: Black and Silver, The New Quixote, Mr. Foot and Chinamen.

These plays were first performed in London by Lynn Redgrave and Richard Briers at the Garrick Theatre on 30th July, 1970, in a Michael Codron production, directed by Mark Cullingham.

Michael Frayn was born in London in 1933 and educated at Kingston Grammar School and Cambridge. He became a reporter for the *Manchester Guardian* and eventually came to write the *Guardian's* 'Miscellany' column. He began writing for the *Observer* in 1962. His first novel 'The Tin Men' was published in 1965 and won for Michael Frayn the coveted Somerset Maugham award. He has since written several novels and television plays.

BLACK AND SILVER

CHARACTERS

HUSBAND

WIFE

SETTING

A hotel bedroom in Venice.

BLACK AND SILVER

Night. HUSBAND *and* WIFE *are asleep. The window is open; reflections of lapping water move tranquilly up the wall outside. The curtain stirs in the night breeze. From somewhere in the distance there is a snatch of song. A church clock strikes three. It is followed by the sound of a small baby starting first to fret and then to cry. At the first serious cry the* WIFE *starts up in bed, eyes still shut. She remains like that for a moment. The baby stops crying. The* WIFE'S *head fall back on to the pillow like a stone. A moment's silence, and then the baby starts to cry again. Once more the* WIFE *sits up in bed. This time she rubs her eyes and opens them; drags her hands down over her face; licks her lips; runs a weary hand through her hair. She sighs, and braces herself with determination as if she is going to get up. Instead she drives her elbow into her* HUSBAND'S *back.*

WIFE. Your turn. (*For a moment nothing happens. Then, in one complete delayed reflex action, the* HUSBAND *rolls straight out of bed on to his feet and heads for the door of the bathroom, his eyes still shut. His* WIFE *falls back on the pillow, asleep.*)

HUSBAND. (*Inarticulately, his voice muscles still anaesthetized by sleep.*) All right! Just going! Leave it to me! Sh! (*A chair carrying the clothes stands between him and the door. He falls over it noisily. The* WIFE *sits up in bed at once.*)

WIFE. (*Whispering.*) Sh! You'll wake the whole hotel!

HUSBAND. (*Blindly picking up himself and the chair, and piling the clothes back on to it.*) Sh! Relax! Leave it all to me! You're supposed to be having a holiday, remember. (*He moves the chair out of harm's way, then opens the bathroom door and pulls out a carry-cot on a conveyor, which he starts to push hurriedly back and forth. The crying stops and the* WIFE *subsides on to her pillow again. The* HUSBAND, *whose eyes are still shut, and whose attitude suggests that he is trying to remain asleep on his feet, gradually ceases his pushing and creeps back to bed. When he gets to where the chair originally was, he stops and makes a careful detour, which brings him up against it in its new position. Once again he falls over it; the baby cries; the* WIFE *starts up accusingly.* HUSBAND *putting the chair back into its original place, and returning to quiet the baby.*) O.K.! Just going! Don't worry! Leave it to me! I'll fix it! Sh! (*He pushes the carry-cot back and forth. The baby quietens.*)

WIFE. If you're going to go crashing about like this all night, you'd better put him back in the bathroom. (*He wheels the cot into the bathroom, and emerges closing the door behind him. He heads back for bed, elaborately avoiding the chair in every possible position.*) He is properly covered up, isn't he?

HUSBAND. (*Reassuringly.*) Yes . . .

WIFE. You did check?

HUSBAND. Yes, yes. (*He gets back into bed and settles down. A pause. The* WIFE *is still sitting up, worrying.*)

WIFE. Has he got a window open in there?

HUSBAND. (*Reassuringly, from the depths of the pillow.*) Mm! Mm! (*A pause.*)

WIFE. There aren't any windows in the bathroom.

HUSBAND. (*Explaining, without waking up.*) Urm urmle urmurmurm . . .

WIFE. What?

HUSBAND. (*Wearily, taking his head out of the pillow.*) I said no, but there's a ventilator. (*A pause.*)

WIFE. Do you think he's getting enough vitamins? (*Sighing, the* HUSBAND *sits up and turns on the light.*) I mean, he brings up all his feed. He must bring up all the vitamins, too, mustn't he? (*The* HUSBAND *looks at his watch.*)

HUSBAND. (*Pleadingly.*) It's three o'clock! (*Offended at the implied rebuke, she turns away from him and lies down.*) We're supposed to be on holiday! We're supposed to be getting some rest and relaxation!

WIFE. Rest and relaxation!

HUSBAND. What?

WIFE. How can I relax when everyone in the restaurant has to look the other way each time he brings his feed up?

HUSBAND. The *Italians* are all right—*they* don't mind him bringing his feed up. The Signora—all the girls who do the rooms—they think he's *marvellous*. It's all these English honeymoon couples. (*He turns the light out and lies down.*)

WIFE. Well, it wasn't my idea, coming back to Venice and getting the room we spent our honeymoon in.

HUSBAND. All they get at this hotel are honeymooners! I don't think they've ever seen a baby before, half of them!

WIFE. I feel like a spectre at the feast, coming into the restaurant with the baby every morning.

HUSBAND. The *Italians* seem to think children are quite natural. '*E, bambolino! O, che bello ragazzo!* Can I hold him? *Eccolo! Bambolino, bambolino, bambolino!* Look—his little hands and foots! I keep him, yes? (*His voice dies away. He has become aware that the baby is crying again. They both lie there, neither making the first move. Then the* WIFE *sits up, sighing. At once the* HUSBAND *sits up, too—resignedly.*) All right! All right! I'm on duty. (*He swings his legs out of bed. The* WIFE *lies down again.*) He's stopped. (*He swings his legs back into bed. Immediately the crying starts again. He swings his legs out of bed, walks slowly and aggrievedly towards the bathroom.*) If you're going to be worn out every day, I suppose on holiday's as good a time as any . . . (*He has reached the bathroom door, and it just about to open it, but realizes that the baby has stopped crying again. He stands stock still for a moment, listening intently. Then he turns on his heel, and heads back towards the bed.*) The only thing that worries me is whether all this doesn't rather make a fool of one—whether it doesn't . . . (*The crying starts again. The* HUSBAND *freezes, and turns back towards the bathroom. The crying stops. He waits a moment, then heads back towards the bed.*) . . . weaken one's personality as . . . (*He stops and swings back towards the bathroom, thinking to get a step ahead in the game. But the baby doesn't cry. He resumes his trip back to bed.*) . . . as a father, in one's . . . (*He gets into bed.*) . . . relationship with the child . . . (*The baby at once starts to cry. This time the* HUSBAND *does nothing, except let his head sink into his hands. The* WIFE *sits up, exasperated, as if the* HUSBAND *had never made any effort at all.*)

WIFE. Are you going, or shall I?

HUSBAND. (*Wearily, getting up again.*) No, no, no! Go to sleep. My round! I'm in the chair! (*He trails to the bathroom, and pulls the carry-cot out, jiggling it back and forth as he does so. The crying dies away. The* WIFE *subsides on to her pillow. Suddenly, he sniffs, and frowns. He stops pushing the cot back and forth; at which the baby starts to cry again; at which the* WIFE *sits up in bed. The* HUSBAND *doesn't notice her, however, because he is bending low over the cot, lifting the blanket within, and sniffing cautiously. He starts up hastily, whereupon the* WIFE *lies down again and feigns immediate sleep. The* HUSBAND *silently curses his luck, then, automatically pushing the cot back and forth to quiet the baby, looks round at her and speaks ingratiatingly.*) Darling . . . ! (*There is no response. He goes over to her, dragging the cot, and his ingratiating tone becomes more urgent.*) It's big jobs. (*There is still no response. He shakes her uncertainly, undecided between firmness and gallantry.*) Well, that's damned funny, I must say. She was awake a moment ago. (*The* HUSBAND *turns to the cot and starts to remove the nappy.*) It's not that I *mind* doing it. It's just that I don't know where she keeps the stuff . . . (*To the baby, in the special upbeat tweedling tones reserved for talking to babies.*) Yes, it's old Dad who's on the job tonight, because lucky old Mum happens to be all tucked up in bed snoring her head off . . . ! Yes, she does . . . ! Oh, what a little stinky lad! What a little pooey-wooey . . . uggy-puggy . . . (*His increasing preoccupation with the difficulties of the operation makes his tone suddenly peremptory.*) No, lie still! Lie *still*, blast you, or you'll get your feet in it! (*He looks round desperately, holding the baby's feet.*) Something to wipe you with . . . (*There is plainly nothing in sight. The baby gurgles contentedly. The* HUSBAND *addresses it in his tweedling voice.*) It's all right for *you* to laugh! Yes, it's all right for *you* to laugh! I said it's all right for *you* to laugh . . . ! (*He looks desperately round again, returning to his more usual irritated adult tones.*) But what the flaming hell has she done with the Kleenex? *I* don't know where she keeps things, do I, boy? (*Still holding the baby's feet up with one hand, he peers into the bathroom.*) She hides them all away in some godforsaken place, so I have to hold your bottom up in the air with one hand . . . (*He sees what he wants, high up inside the bathroom, and reaches off impossibly for it, still holding the baby's feet.*) . . . and with the other . . . do my best to . . . (*The sentence is completed by a cascading crash of falling objects, which makes the* WIFE *sit up and put the light on, and brings her jumping out of bed and running to intervene. She gazes into the bathroom at her* HUSBAND's *efforts. He speaks defensively.*) Well, fancy putting the Kleenex up on the topmost shelf!

WIFE. For God's sake! The whole of Venice must be awake by now!

HUSBAND. (*Sarcastically.*) Do you usually change the baby up on the top shelf!

WIFE. (*Fetching both Kleenex and a clean paper nappy*

from the wreckage in the bathroom.) Go back to bed. I'll finish this.

HUSBAND. (*Trying to keep her away from the cot.*) No, no, no—I'll do it. You're supposed to be having a holiday.

WIFE. Some holiday . . .

HUSBAND. Anyway, I'm doing it. You go back to bed and get some sleep.

WIFE. Sleep! I've forgotten what the word means! I wouldn't know it if I saw it! Come on, out of there. (*She brushes him out of the way and finishes changing the baby.*)

HUSBAND. (*Watching aggrievedly.*) I don't know why you're so eager all of a sudden.

WIFE. (*Tweedlingly, to baby.*) Was it a nasty terrible surprise seeing that horrible Daddy man changing your nappy? (*Fiercely, to* HUSBAND.) Because you make such a bloody meal of it!

HUSBAND. *You* put the Kleenex out of reach!

WIFE. (*Tweedlingly, to baby.*) Is he keeping you awake, too, then, throwing all the jars of Nappisan and all the packets of Bickiepegs and all the little tins of Heinz strained spinach round the bathroom? (*Fiercely, to* HUSBAND.) I don't know why you're so eager all of a sudden, come to that.

HUSBAND. Because I don't see why you should store up all the credit for changing his nappy when I've done all the dirty work already, that's why!

WIFE. This is the third time I've been up tonight.

HUSBAND. It's the third time *I've* been up.

WIFE. I was up most of last night.

HUSBAND. Who cleared up the mess in the Doge's Palace?

WIFE. (*Turning on him indignantly.*) I like that! What about the St. Mark's incident . . . ?

HUSBAND. (*Suddenly conciliating.*) Oh, come on—let's not fight. (*He sits down on the bed. The* WIFE *turns back to finish the baby, agreeing to be slightly mollified.*)

We had a great fight on our honeymoon. I can remember standing looking out of that window at the canal and thinking our marriage was over. I can't remember what we were arguing about, though. What on earth *did* we argue about before *he* was born? What did we talk about? What did we think about? We must have been bored out of our minds . . . Do you remember that day we went out to Torcello and had a drink at the hotel where Hemingway used to stay? And you picked one of their geraniums and pinned it on my shirt . . . ? (*She turns to him, smiling slightly, and hands him the soiled nappy. He looks at it tenderly, rather as if it were a geranium, and puts his hands around hers.*)

WIFE. Put it down the lavatory for me, will you?

HUSBAND. Oh . . . Right. (*He takes it out to the bathroom. She is just bending over the cot again when a sudden thought strikes her.*)

WIFE. Peter! Remember not to turn on the hot water!

HUSBAND. (*Off.*) What?

WIFE. The hot water! (*A colossal thumping of air-locked plumbing fills the night. At once the baby starts to cry. The* WIFE's *head droops. She takes the baby out of the cot, wrapped up in its shawl, and gets back into bed with it, cradling it. It stops crying. She turns out the light. The* HUSBAND *comes out of the bathroom, drying his hands. He seizes the cot and pushes it out to the bathroom, addressing a few encouraging words to the interior of the cot on the way.*)

HUSBAND. Straight off to sleep now! There's a good boy! (*The* WIFE *dozes off. The* HUSBAND *executes a cunning retreat from the bathroom, then stands outside the door and listens. He smiles at the silence, and begins to creep away. But before he has gone more than a step or two he stops, frowning. He goes back and listens again. He frowns anxiously. He bends closer to the door and listens more intently. Then he pulls the cot out of the bathroom and puts his ear right down on top of it. He turns appalled to his* WIFE, *and says in a terrible panic-*

stricken whisper.) I think he's stopped breathing! (*The* WIFE *at once wakes with a start, and, still carrying the baby, jumps out of bed and runs to join the* HUSBAND. *She bends over the cot to listen.*) I mean, I don't want to wake him up if he *is* breathing . . .

WIFE. (*Urgently.*) Hold this . . . (*She hands the baby to the* HUSBAND, *and pulls back the covers from the cot. She panics completely.*) Oh, my God, he's not there! (WIFE *and* HUSBAND *stare at each other for an instant in horror. But at that moment the baby gives a cry, and they both become aware of its whereabouts. The* WIFE *snatches it out of the* HUSBAND'S *arms, with a look at him which suggests that he was attempting to murder it. She hugs and kisses it and puts it back into the cot. Reaction to their shock makes them both furious.*) Stupid trick to play!

HUSBAND. Well, it wasn't my fault!

WIFE. Not breathing!

HUSBAND. Well, he *wasn't* breathing there—he was breathing somewhere else! (*They both get grumpily back into bed. The* WIFE *has pulled the cot up to her side of the bed, so that she can keep jiggling it back and forth as she lies there. The* HUSBAND *remains sitting up in bed with his arms round his knees.*) Well, I'm wide awake now. I couldn't go to sleep if you paid me . . . (*There is no response from the* WIFE.) You realize it's not breakfast time for another five hours yet? You didn't pack any jigsaw puzzles, did you? (*No response. A faint, rhythmic squeaking of springs becomes audible.*) What's that?

WIFE. What?

HUSBAND. That squeak, squeak. (*The* WIFE *stops pushing the cot to and fro for a moment and listens.*)

WIFE. Oh, that's the couple next door. (*The* HUSBAND *frowns, puzzled. Then light dawns.*)

HUSBAND. You mean, they've got a baby in there, too? Pushing it back and forth like us? (*The* WIFE *just looks at him.*) I thought they were all honeymoon couples

in the hotel, apart from us? (*The* WIFE *goes on staring.*)
Oh . . . ! But at three o'clock in the morning?

WIFE. We probably woke them up. Anyway, why not?

HUSBAND. Well . . . ! (*He thinks.*) I suppose we used
to make love in the middle of the night, sometimes.
Didn't we? I can't remember. It all seems so long ago.

WIFE. I can't remember what it was like at all before
he was born.

HUSBAND. What did we do with all that time?

WIFE. We used to go to the cinema. Didn't we? Twice
a week sometimes.

HUSBAND. We went out for meals in Chinese restau-
rants.

WIFE. We stayed in bed on Sundays . . . (*The squeaking has ceased. The* WIFE *stops jiggling the cot, and turns
to the* HUSBAND.) Oh, Peter! What's happened to us?
Have we changed? Have I changed? I have, haven't I?

HUSBAND. (*Reassuringly.*) No, you haven't. (*He puts
his arm round her.*)

WIFE. Do you still love me?

HUSBAND. Of course I do. (*He squeezes her affection-
ately.*)

WIFE. But not just out of habit? Not just out of a
sense of duty?

HUSBAND. (*Stroking her head.*) No!

WIFE. I still . . . you know . . . *attract* you? (*He
kisses her mouth, and silences her.*) Even though I'm so
preoccupied with him . . . ? (*He kisses her again.*) . . .
and so ill-tempered and . . . ? (*He kisses her again,
pressing her back on to the pillow.*) . . . so on? (*She
gazes up at him in silence.*) We'll have to be very quiet,
then . . . (*Just as he is about to kiss her again, the baby
starts to fret. They both freeze. The* HUSBAND *looks
round murderously at the cot.*) Oh . . . Never mind! Go
on! (*The* HUSBAND *continues to stare at the cot. The
baby falls silent again. Slowly the* HUSBAND *turns back
to kiss his* WIFE. *She puts her arm round him. Once again*

the baby begins to cry. Once again the HUSBAND *looks round desperately. Without letting go of the* HUSBAND, *the* WIFE *stretches out her arm and begins to push the cot back and forth. The crying stops. Still pushing, she tries to encourage her* HUSBAND.) I love you!

HUSBAND. (*Doing his best to concentrate on her.*) I love you!

WIFE. Go on, then! Don't stop! (*But he turns to look at the cot, then disengages himself from her and sits up gloomily.*)

HUSBAND. I'll wait till you've got him back to sleep again. (*He lies back against the pillows beside her. She sighs, and takes his hand.*)

WIFE. I'm sorry, love . . . I'm sorry. I feel it's all my fault. (*They lie side by side, gazing in front of them, hand in hand, she pushing the cot back and forth. Gradually his head begins to loll, and his eyes close.*) Do you remember that day right at the end of the honeymoon, when we came back across the Lagoon in the twilight in that man's old motorboat, and the water was absolutely still—all black and silver, black and silver—and we dropped anchor and swam and the water was so warm and dark that you felt you could just let yourself go, and drift down into it forever . . . ? (*She turns and sees that his eyes are shut.*) You're not going to sleep? Are you? (*His head slips a little further sideways.*) I thought we were going to . . . Peter! (*She prods him sharply. There is a momentary pause, and then, in one complete delayed reflex action, he rolls straight out of bed on to his feet, as at the beginning, and heads for where the cot was, his eyes still shut.*)

HUSBAND. (*Inarticulately.*) All right! Just going! Sh! Leave it to me . . . ! (*BLACKOUT, as he once again falls over the chair, and the baby cries.*)

THE NEW QUIXOTE

CHARACTERS

GINA

KENNETH

SETTING

The living-room of Gina's tiny one-up one-down urban cottage. Once, presumably, it housed a tiny artisan and his ten tiny children. Now, from its decoration and furnishing, it houses a single lady with taste, professional salary, and firmly-set neat ways. A front door opens direct from the street; another door gives access to the stairs and everything else.

THE NEW QUIXOTE

The room is empty, and half-dark, the only light coming around the drawn curtains at the window. Somewhere church bells are ringing. The stairs door opens, and GINA *enters, yawning and pulling a dressing-gown over her nightdress. She draws the curtains, blinking in the light, and looks at her watch.*)

GINA. Quarter to eleven . . . Oh God—Sundays! (*She goes to the front door, takes in a Sunday paper and a single pint of milk, and crosses towards the stairs door.*) Waste, waste, waste, waste, waste . . . (*She stops just as she is about to go out, realising that she has seen something out of place. She puts down the papers and the milk, and goes back to pick up a drab-coloured plastic mac lying across one of the armchairs. She stares at it, puzzled, then sees that lying beneath it is a small, shabby, brown rucksack. She picks this up, too. The flap is open. She pulls out a thermos flask, a couple of heavy reference books, and a slide rule. She stares at the objects, then round the room, baffled. Then suddenly she remembers. She catches her breath and claps a hand to her mouth, then laughs guiltily at herself.*) Oh, dear! Oh, Lordy! Forgotten all about him! (*Giggling guiltily, she goes to the stairs door and calls, rather uncertainly.*) Um . . . hello . . . ! Are you still here, then . . . ? Are you in the bathroom, um . . . ? (*She looks inside the flap of the rucksack.*) . . . K.B. Prosser Esquire? Keith? (*No reply. She closes the door, and stands there thoughtfully.*) Or was it Kenneth? He had a van, didn't he? (*She goes to the front door, and looks out.*) Gone . . . Oh, dear! Never just forgotten all about it before. That really is beginning to get a bit sleazy. (*She gives a very*

19

*small laugh, more shocked at herself than she would like
to admit. She turns it into a joke, and smacks her hand.*)
Smack, smack, smack! If it happens again—the head-
mistress! (*She looks at the raincoat and rucksack.*) I'd
better post them on—I don't suppose he'll feel much like
coming back for them now . . . Brown paper, while I
think of it . . . (*She goes out through the stairs door,
closing it behind her. At once a key turns in the front
door, and* KENNETH *enters. He is in his twenties, and is
wearing spectacles, an open-necked shirt, a shapeless
sports jacket with a row of pens in the breast-pocket, and
brown corduroy trousers. From his appearance you sus-
pect at once that he collects train numbers, or plays
chess, or is a radio ham. He is in fact carrying a load of
electronic equipment—the uncased elements of a home-
made stereophonic rig. He spreads them over the neat
period furniture and plugs them in. Then he goes quietly
across to the stairs door and listens. Reassured by the
silence, he walks lightly back to the front door, and
carries in a couple of loudspeakers and an armful of
records. He connects up the loudspeakers and puts on a
record. The room is at once filled with Messiaen, played
at full stereo enthusiast's loudness. He opens the stairs
door to let the sound out in that direction, then goes out
of the front door again, very pleased with himself.* GINA
*comes running in through the stairs door, astonished and
terrified. She gazes round the room with incomprehen-
sion, covers her ears, and runs to the control panel, trying
to find some way of turning it off.* KENNETH *comes in
through the front door, carrying another load of records
and books. At the sight of* GINA *he puts them down and
runs to embrace her. She backs away, appalled. They
shout to each other inaudibly over the noise.*)
  KENNETH. Darling!
  GINA. What? What is all this?
  KENNETH. I thought I'd give you a surprise! An
aubade!
  GINA. What?

KENNETH. A morning song!

GINA. What? (*She gestures to him to turn the sound down. He does so.*)

KENNETH. To serenade you awake! Like Wagner playing the Siegfried Idyll to Cosima!

GINA. Well, listen, Keith . . .

KENNETH. Kenneth.

GINA. I mean Kenneth.

KENNETH. Keith! (*Laughing at her mistake, he kisses her again. As he does so, he stretches out a hand and turns up the gramophone full blast again. Shouting.*) It's so fantastically sensual!

GINA. (*Shouting.*) Look, what is all this? What's going on?

KENNETH. (*Shouting.*) It's Messiaen! Messiaen! (*He turns the sound down.*) Messiaen! Turangalila, by Messiaen!

GINA. What?

KENNETH. We were talking about it last night. At the party. When we were sitting on the stairs. You remember! You just suddenly said how you liked Messiaen.

GINA. Did I?

KENNETH. I couldn't believe my ears! To meet someone like you who knew about Messiaen! I thought I couldn't have heard right over the noise! I just kept saying, 'You like Messiaen?'

GINA. And what did I say?

KENNETH. You just . . . nodded and smiled . . .

GINA. Oh. That was the bit when I was nodding and smiling?

KENNETH. You kept nodding and smiling all the time! Oh, Gina! Supposing we hadn't met! Supposing you'd just decided to have an early night instead of going to the party!

GINA. Yes . . .

KENNETH. You'd be sitting here. I'd be sitting in my little room . . .

GINA. I thought you *had* gone, as a matter of fact.

KENNETH. Gone? Gone where?

GINA. Well, back to your . . . little room, or whatever. (*He laughs at her tenderly, and kisses her.*)

KENNETH. Oh, you silly girl! I just went to fetch my stuff! (*He goes out of the front door.*)

GINA. Your stuff! What stuff! (*He reappears with a suitcase and a couple of suits on hangers.*)

KENNETH. I didn't take long in the van. I don't believe in loading myself with a lot of personal possessions. (*He goes out again.*)

GINA. Before you fetch anything else in, Keith . . . (*He reappears carrying a number of pictures, and a polythene bag full of washing, smiling at her mistake.*)

KENNETH. Kenneth! (*He shuts the front door.*) That's the lot. Wherever my stereo and records are—that's home.

GINA. Kenneth, I think we'd better sit down quietly and have a serious talk.

KENNETH. I just want to talk and talk all day! (*They sit down.*) I've got so many things I must tell you! Oh, Gina!

GINA. Now, Kenneth . . .

KENNETH. You can call me Keith if you want to. I don't feel like Kenneth any more! I feel completely changed! As if I was walking about in a story, and it was all written down already! Do you know what I mean! It's like seeing the world for the first time! That chair, for instance—it's *beautiful!*

GINA. That chair? I should think it was—I paid £60 for it. Now, listen, Kenneth, I don't want you to think I regret last night, or that I didn't enjoy it . . .

KENNETH. I never guessed what it could be like! I've only known girls of my own age before!

GINA. Well, that's another thing . . .

KENNETH. I didn't get to sleep at all! I couldn't believe it had happened! When it started to get light I got up and sat by the window for an hour, just looking out. Cars standing waiting all down the street. Covered with dew—

dew all over their windscreens, as if their eyes were shut. Everything still. Just so. Just right. All written down already. Then I came and sat on the floor next to the bed, and looked at you. You were lying on your side, with your hair all over the pillow. (*Instinctively she puts her hand up to it.*) Every time you breathed out, it stirred the down at the corner of your mouth. You've got a faint, faint moustache—I hadn't realised. (*She puts her hand over her upper lip.*) No—I love it! I stroked it. Didn't you feel it in your sleep? I kissed the wrinkles at the corner of your eye. (*She gets up and goes over to the window.*)

GINA. I'm sorry about them.

KENNETH. I felt I wanted to cry.

GINA. About the wrinkles?

KENNETH. About you. Or about me. I knew all the first part of my life was over, all the silly bit. Now the serious part was starting.

GINA. Oh, dear!

KENNETH. Anyway, I decided to go and get my stuff, and move in properly before you woke up. I just quickly got dressed, and took the doorkey out of your bag. Mum was waiting in the hall when I came in—I've been living at home, you see. She said: 'Where have you been, Kenneth?' 'Oh—friend's house.' (*He laughs at the inadequacy of this formula.* GINA *gazes at him uneasily.*) So I put the stuff in the van, and she said, 'Where are you going, then, Kenneth?' And I said, 'Oh—moving in with my friend.' And she said, 'Aren't you going to have some breakfast before you go?' And I said, 'No—I'll have breakfast there.' And that was that. All that part of my life—finished.

GINA. (*Dismayed.*) Oh, my dear sweet boy! What have you done?

KENNETH. And all the way back I thought, 'Now I can do anything! Nothing can touch me now!' And I drove on the wrong side of the road, and went into a roundabout at forty! I must have been mad! I couldn't steer! The back of the van skidded round and crashed into the wall! Then I thought, 'Oh God, I'm going to get killed before I can tell her about everything!' Because I wanted to tell you about the cars with dew on the windscreen, and about how I used to cycle to school, and how you looked when you were asleep, and . . . and how the world is really completely different from what you think, and how everything's going to be all right. I wanted to say it all at once, in a great shout, but I couldn't think of the words. So I thought, I'll just creep in with the stereo, and I'll say *this* . . . (*He turns up the Messiaen full blast. Then he takes her hand and sits on the floor in front of her, gazing up at her. She laughs, touched in spite of herself. Then she gestures for the sound to be turned down. He does so.*)

GINA. Well, now you've said it.

KENNETH. Yes.

GINA. And I feel . . . very touched. But now let's just be serious for a moment, shall we? (*He begins to pace up and down excitedly.*)

KENNETH. I haven't even begun to tell you how I *feel* about everything! It's so complicated and surprising! I think what I feel most of all is . . . (*He stops to examine his feelings.*) Completely exhausted! (*He slumps into the sofa, almost as if he is going to faint. She gazes at him.*)

GINA. I'll make you some breakfast.

KENNETH. (*Palely, without rising.*) I'll do it. You sit down. (*She laughs, and goes out through the stairs door.*)

GINA. (*Off.*) Toast and coffee and orange-juice all right? (*He nods, and stretches himself out full-length.*) What?

KENNETH. (*Faintly.*) Yes, fine . . . Oh, dear! Oh dear oh dear . . . ! (*He closes his eyes and falls instantly asleep.* GINA *re-enters carrying two glasses of orange-juice.*)

GINA. Now, drink this up and you'll feel a lot better. (*She sits down on the edge of the sofa, and sets his orange-juice down on the floor beside him.*) Now, Kenneth, be a good boy and listen to what I'm going to say very carefully, and don't misunderstand me. I like you very much, Kenneth, and I hope we shall see quite a lot of each other. But I don't think we ought to rush our fences. I'm a lot older than you . . . (*He snorts in his sleep.*) Well, I am. You're very young and impulsive—full of enthusiasm for life . . . (*He snores. She looks round at him.*) Oh, *no!* Oh, *Lord!* If you can't hear what's been said at parties, never, never, never nod and smile! (*She gets up and picks up the record sleeve.*) Messiaen . . . ! I might have guessed it would be something like that we were talking about. (*She looks down at him.*) What was I like at that age? I didn't go around behaving like this! (*She bends close to examine his face, frowning. She feels his upper lip, then her own. She feels the corners of his eyes, and then the corners of her own eyes.*) It won't do, will it? Look at all this stuff? Picasso prints! Oh, heavens! A bag of dirty washing! That's for me, I suppose. (*In a funny voice.*) 'It's no good—he'll have to go.' (*She turns up the Messiaen full blast. He stirs, half-opens his eyes, and smiles at her. She turns the sound down again, and sits down on the edge of the sofa.*) Are you properly awake?

KENNETH. Um. (*He sits up, puts his arm round her, and pulls her down on top of him. She struggles free.*)

GINA. No, no, no! We've got to be serious for a moment. Have a drink of orange-juice and clear your head. (*She hands him the glass. He drinks, dazed.*) One thing we must get straight at once, Kenneth. You can't stay here.

KENNETH. Oh, sorry, Gina. I'll move upstairs into the bed.

GINA. No, I mean you can't just *move in* like this!

KENNETH. (*Baffled.*) Why not?

GINA. Well, because . . . because you can't! I haven't invited you to, have I?

KENNETH. How long have I been asleep? What's been

happening? When I went to sleep everything was new and different. I wake up and it's all back to normal again.

GINA. I'm sorry, Kenneth.

KENNETH. We love each other, don't we?

GINA. Well . . .

KENNETH. I love you. You love me. Don't you?

GINA. Well . . .

KENNETH. Of course you do, Gina! You said you did, last night.

GINA. Did I?

KENNETH. Yes!

GINA. On the stairs, was this? Nodding and smiling?

KENNETH. In bed!

GINA. Oh . . . *then* . . .

KENNETH. Yes, then!

GINA. But supposing somebody comes in?

KENNETH. Who?

GINA. Well, a friend . . .

KENNETH. That's all right. I shan't be embarrassed . . . What sort of friend?

GINA. Well, let's say a man. Someone coming to take me out.

KENNETH. (*Staring at her.*) You've got men who . . . take you out?

GINA. Well, yes. I'm not *that* old, am I?

KENNETH. You never told me that.

GINA. You never asked.

KENNETH. But you wouldn't let them . . . take you out *now*.

GINA. How do you mean, *now?*

KENNETH. I mean, after . . . well, *now.*

GINA. What do you want me to do, Kenneth? Ring them all up and tell them not to call?

KENNETH. How many of them are there?

GINA. Well, I don't know—I don't keep a list . . .

KENNETH. But there are several?

GINA. Yes!

KENNETH. Not just one special one?

GINA. No! Well . . . yes.

KENNETH. There *is* a special one?

GINA. Yes.

KENNETH. Someone you used to be in love with?

GINA. *Used* to be in love with?

KENNETH. Before.

GINA. Well . . . someone I'm . . . fond of.

KENNETH. But not in love with?

GINA. Look, he's someone I've known for a long time. I don't want to hurt his feelings. He'll be very upset if he comes in through that door and finds you and all your stuff in occupation.

KENNETH. He's not coming today, is he?

GINA. Well, he may!

KENNETH. Oh, God—I should never have gone to sleep!

GINA. As a matter of fact he is. He's coming to take me out to lunch.

KENNETH. You must explain to him, then, love!

GINA. Now, Kenneth, be a good boy . . .

KENNETH. *I'll* explain to him!

GINA. Oh, Kenneth! We'll see each other next week some time.

KENNETH. What sort of man is he? Older than me?

GINA. Yes.

KENNETH. Is he . . . handsome?

GINA. Yes.

KENNETH. What kind of work does he do?

GINA. He . . . works for one of those big oil companies.

KENNETH. What's his name?

GINA. Lionel.

KENNETH. Lionel . . . Where's he taking you for lunch?

GINA. *I* don't know!

KENNETH. What sort of places does he usually take you to? Expensive places?

GINA. Sometimes.

KENNETH. The Ritz? The Dorchester? Places like that?

GINA. More or less.

KENNETH. Night clubs?

GINA. Occasionally. (*He continues to stare at her. Then suddenly he laughs and relaxes.*)

KENNETH. Oh, Gina, darling! For a moment I thought you were being serious! (*He kisses her. She gazes at him in astonishment.*) I'm going to get the breakfast. I'm starving.

GINA. Kenneth . . .

KENNETH. No, no—you sit down. You must be tired, too. I'm very good in the kitchen. Tomorrow I'll bring you breakfast in bed. (*Solicitously he turns up the Messiaen full blast, blows her another kiss, and goes out through the stairs door. She gazes after him in astonishment.*)

GINA. (*Shouting.*) I am being serious! Oh, damn this noise! (*She turns down the gramophone.*) I am serious! Why do you think I'm not? (*He reappears in the doorway, holding the butter-knife.*)

KENNETH. (*With amused gentleness.*) Women don't fall in love with handsome men who take them to night-clubs! Where's the butter?

GINA. (*Bemused.*) In the cupboard over the sink. (*He disappears again.*) Don't they? (*He reappears, holding the butter.*)

KENNETH. Well, some women may. But *you* don't, Gina, love, you silly girl! (*He kisses her neck.*) *You* fall in love with scruffy, short-sighted men like me, who work for obscure electronics firms, and arrive with all their dirty washing in a plastic bag. Sit down, darling . . . (*She sits down, unable to think of a reply. He goes out of the door again.*)

GINA. What we've got to bear in mind, Kenneth, is Lionel's feelings. We have known each other a very long time, you see. He's very jealous. When he comes in and sees you . . . and all this dirty washing, and so on . . . he'll go crazy, he really will. (KENNETH *enters, holding the coffee-pot.*)

KENNETH. I really don't think he cares for you very much, Gina.

GINA. How do you know? You haven't met him!

KENNETH. If he really cared for you he wouldn't have to fling himself about in jealous rages, would he? I'm not flinging myself about in a jealous rage. He's just trying to prove to himself that he really loves you. That's why he takes you to all those night clubs and places! The more demonstrative someone is, the more he's trying to cover up for his real lack of feeling underneath.

GINA. He may hit you, or something.

KENNETH. Exactly!

GINA. He may . . . break your gramophone!

KENNETH. I shan't let him do that, I'm afraid. I built that stereo myself.

GINA. You may not be able to stop him! He's very . . . powerfully built.

KENNETH. The tougher they look on the surface, the softer they are underneath. Where's the sugar?

GINA. Same place as the butter. (*He goes out again.*) The softer they look on the surface, the tougher they are to get rid of. (*He reappears, carrying coffee and toast for them both on a tray.*)

KENNETH. I can find my way round your kitchen without any trouble at all.

GINA. So I see.

KENNETH. Sit down, love. (*She sits, reluctantly, then attempts to pour the coffee.*) No, no, I'll do it! White? I like being in your kitchen. Lots of dark red flowery things. All the white bits just the right shade of white— not too clinical. Everything quietly in its place. Everything just so . . . I have tried living with a girl once before, as a matter of fact.

GINA. Really? Was she surprised?

KENNETH. It was terrible. She shared the flat with

two other girls. They all used to wash their hair in the kitchen sink. They dried their stockings over the breakfast table. (*She sighs.*) Tired?

GINA. A little weary, in some ways.

KENNETH. Like some music?

GINA. No, no, no.

KENNETH. I know—I'll feed you. (*He kneels up in front of her and tries to feed her buttered toast. She waves it away.*) No?

GINA. I don't think I'm hungry after all.

KENNETH. I'm not sure I am, either. I feel so strange! Disembodied! As if today it was a completely different world, where there were just words, and feelings, and no one's feet quite touched the ground . . . I went all over the house during the night, when I couldn't sleep. Did you hear me? Do you know what I was doing? I was smelling everywhere.

GINA. You remind me of someone. I wish I could think who.

KENNETH. I smelt you. I smelt your clothes. Then I went and smelt the bathroom. You can always tell what someone's like by the smell of the bathroom. Don't you think so?

GINA. What am I like, then?

KENNETH. I can't say it—I can only smell it. The whole house smelt good, Gina. Neat, tidy. You could smell the clock ticking.

GINA. You do remind me of someone. Perhaps it's someone I saw in a dream.

KENNETH. I know why you told me all that stuff about Lionel. I know why you were trying to get rid of me.

GINA. What? I wasn't trying to get rid of you, exactly. I was just trying to . . .

KENNETH. You just suddenly felt you couldn't stand the sight of me another minute.

GINA. No, no . . .

KENNETH. Don't worry! I know how it is sometimes.

You get afraid of your own feelings. They seem so huge
and uncontrollable—you don't know where they're going
to take you. In a way, the stronger your feelings are, the
more you want to deny them. Every time I look at you
and see No, no, no! in your eyes—oh, I'm not blind, I
can see it there sometimes!—every time I see you looking
No, no, no! I realise it actually means Yes, yes, yes!

GINA. I see.

KENNETH. (*Smiling tenderly.*) You're doing it now!

GINA. Oh am I? Really? (*She turns her eyes away
from him, confused.*)

KENNETH. Don't worry! I know what you really
mean! (*He kisses her hand.*)

GINA. This idea you've got that everything's the opposite of what it seems . . .

KENNETH. Yes!

GINA. You seem to be rather taken with it.

KENNETH. Yes, I am!

GINA. Are you sure you've got it right?

KENNETH. It sounds crazy, doesn't it? (*He laughs.*)
But as a matter of fact it's my . . . sort of . . . philos-
ophy of life. Don't laugh about it! We shouldn't have
met each other without it!

GINA. Shouldn't we?

KENNETH. I got to the party last night, and saw you
almost as soon as I came through the door. You were
standing on the other side of the room, talking to someone, smiling slightly . . . You looked so self-contained
and unapproachable!

GINA. So you approached?

KENNETH. Yes! I knew you were looking like that
just to protect yourself, because you were really very
sweet and soft-hearted and vulnerable. It's taken me years
to work it out! All the girls I met at parties always
seemed to keep smiling distantly and shaking their heads
and looking over my shoulder at somebody else. I thought
there was something wrong with *me!* I didn't realise that
every time they yawned they were really saying yes!

GINA. How *do* you say no, then?

KENNETH. By saying yes! That's what they all thought *I* was doing when I tried to grab their hands, and asked if I could take them home afterwards!

GINA. (*Faintly.*) More coffee?

KENNETH. (*His mind still on the girls.*) Yes, please. (*She goes to pour it, uncertainly. He does not pay any attention to her.*) I mean, no thanks. (*She pours it, and he accepts it absent-mindedly.*) Then I started reading Freud. It was like a revelation! Whatever you seem to be on the surface, it's because you're trying to suppress the opposite inside! You're trying not to admit the inadmissible! You're overcompensating! Well, then it all fell into place! All the books I'd read! All the plays I'd seen! What's the whole of modern literature about, from beginning to end? It's about how everything's not what it seems to be! You start with someone who seems to be a hero—and it turns out in the end that he was really a coward all the time. He looks respectable—he turns out to be a criminal. Looks happy—turns out to be miserable. The sane insane—the insane saner than the sane. If it's bad it's good, and if it's good it's bad. It's all obvious as soon as you see it!

GINA. So now you go to parties and look for hard-faced women with scornful smiles . . . ?

KENNETH. Yes! And instead of saying, 'When can I see you again?' I just stand there looking helpless and saying I haven't got a bed for the night.

GINA. And at once they sense the hidden masculinity?

KENNETH. Well, people like to work things out for themselves, don't they!

GINA. (*Wryly.*) I suppose they like to have new personalities discovered inside them, too.

KENNETH. Yes, they do.

GINA. It always works, does it?

KENNETH. Well, last night was the first time, really. But crumbs! What a first time! (*He kisses her enthusiastically, and begins to pace up and down the room.*) But it's not just people, you see, Gina. It's everything! It's a general theory for understanding the whole universe! You look at this, and you think, this is a chair. But you look into it more closely and you'll see it's not a chair at all. It's a mass of tiny spinning particles! And what about the particles? Are they really and truly particles? Of course not—they're not particles at all! They're electricity! They're energy! Matter is energy!

GINA. (*Gently.*) You're a nut, on top of everything else. Aren't you! A real full-blown nut.

KENNETH. The nuttier it all seems, the more reasonable it actually is. Look at this piece of empty air in front of us. Well, of course, it's not empty. It's a mixture of nitrogen and oxygen, with a proportion of water vapour and carbon dioxide, and traces of argon, neon, helium, krypton, and xenon. It's also polluted with industrial emission gases. It's laden with pollen. It's alive with bacteria. It's full of voices and music from radio stations! Voices speaking high and low; shouting, muttering, singing, sobbing, talking Swahili, Lithuanian, Berber, Welsh, Dutch, Malay! It's crossed by cosmic rays from space; by rays of light from Arcturus, Betelgeuse, and the Crab Nebula; and by faint, faint radio waves from galaxies receding almost at the speed of light on the very edge of the universe! All here, in this piece of empty air between the two of us!

GINA. (*Tenderly.*) But you look so sweet, with the light flashing on your spectacles like that . . .

KENNETH. What?

GINA. Are you really all hard and grown-up underneath?

KENNETH. Well, I think in a crisis . . . You can see from books and plays that it takes a crisis to bring out the truth. If you went through life without a crisis you might never find out what anything was like at all.

GINA. And your collar open, and your arms waving about . . .

KENNETH. But the thing is, Gina, the implications of

all this! Because, you see, if right's wrong, and bad's good, and energy's matter, and a chair isn't a chair—then the whole structure of logic collapses! The whole of mathematics! The very possibility of organised thought . . . ! (*He stops in mid-stride, suddenly realising that she is crying.*) Gina! What's the matter? (*He runs to comfort her.*) Oh, sweetest! Never mind! Logic and mathematics don't matter all that much! We'll get by without them! We've got on all right up to now! Perhaps I was exaggerating a bit, anyway. It might be possible to think some thoughts.

GINA. I've just suddenly remembered who it as you remind me of. It *was* someone in a dream. I dreamt once I had a son. He was grown-up already in my dream—he was a young man. And he walked up and down, with the neck of his shirt open, full of ideas, so bright and quick and excited by everything . . .

KENNETH. It proves I'm right, though, doesn't it! There we were yesterday with you self-possessed and me helpless; and here we are today with you in tears and me comforting you.

GINA. Unless I made the whole dream up when I saw you . . .

KENNETH. My moving in—that was the crisis. I told you you had to have a crisis, didn't I!

GINA. I don't suppose I shall ever have a son now. My life hasn't turned out like that.

KENNETH. Don't be sad. I'll look after you. I'll cook the dinner and bring you breakfast in bed.

GINA. (*Stroking his head.*) Poor old Kenneth!

KENNETH. No, poor old Gina!

GINA. Me weeping on your shoulder like this.

KENNETH. I knew you would. I knew as soon as I saw you.

GINA. You poor boy! You sweet boy! You sweet poor kind boy!

KENNETH. Don't worry about your friend Lionel. I'll

deal with him. Have him crying on my other shoulder in
no time.

GINA. There isn't any Lionel. There isn't anyone
coming.

KENNETH. You made him up?

GINA. Sort of.

KENNETH. I knew there was something wrong with
him!

GINA. There's no one I'm really fond of.

KENNETH. I told you, didn't I? As soon as you started
saying he was powerfully built, and very demonstrative,
and so on. I said at once, 'There's something she's trying
to cover up.'

GINA. I felt I had to get you out of here.

KENNETH. I know you did.

GINA. All your stuff . . . I felt almost hysterical!

KENNETH. The more hysterical you got, the more I
knew what you really felt.

GINA. You knew?

KENNETH. Yes.

GINA. All the time?

KENNETH. Yes.

GINA. *I* didn't know!

KENNETH. I know you didn't.

GINA. I really thought I wanted you to go! I thought
you were intolerable!

KENNETH. (*Smiling.*) Yes.

GINA. Bumptious, half-baked . . .

KENNETH. Crack-brained, unfeeling . . .

GINA. That's what I thought. Or that's what I thought
I thought.

KENNETH. Yes, whatever you're thinking, it's never
what you think you're thinking.

GINA. No, I see that now. I was feeling what I seemed
to be feeling just to stop myself feeling what I didn't
know I was feeling.

KENNETH. It's as simple as that.

GINA. It was only when I saw you walking up and

down . . . waving your arms about . . . so excited . . . like a little boy . . . (*She starts to cry again.*)

KENNETH. Sh! Oh, Gina, this has been the most wonderful day of my life. I can't tell you what it's like, suddenly having all your ideas proved like this! It doesn't usually work out so neatly. I've spent weeks and months with unapproachable girls sometimes, trying to get through. Knowing it was there underneath. But finding it was buried so deep you could never get through . . . (*She strokes his head.*) But you just have to have faith. You just have to go on and try again. I got knocked unconscious once.

GINA. By a girl?

KENNETH. By a man. Outside a pub. He kept grabbing hold of people and shouting 'Want a fight, then?' I knew he was really a coward. So I just went up to him, and looked him straight in the eye, and he hit me in the stomach.

GINA. Oh, poor love!

KENNETH. Well, it proved my point, of course. But I cracked my head open on the edge of the pavement. Had to have five stitches.

GINA. Well, now I'm going to look after you, and everything's going to be different. I shan't let anyone yawn at you, or hit you in the stomach.

KENNETH. That's the terrible thing, *knowing you're right* when everyone else can plainly see you're wrong!

GINA. I'm going to feed you up. You're so thin! What was she giving you, that mother of yours? We'll have a proper Sunday lunch for a start. (*She kisses him, and goes to the bag of washing.*) Now where's all this washing that needs to be done?

KENNETH. *Knowing you're right,* when everything around you definitely proves you're wrong! That's the terrible thing!

GINA. Do you like a little starch in your collars? Oh dear, button off here . . .

KENNETH. Well, it's the marvellous thing, really. Because that's how you know you're right! The whole history of the world has been made up of people who were *obviously wrong*, who turned out in the end to be right!

GINA. Some of these pants seem a bit saggy round the waist . . .

KENNETH. It's when something's obviously right that you have to start worrying! When people start taking you seriously! When everything seems to fit!

GINA. Shall I see if I can put some new elastic in for you? (*He does not answer, lost in thought. She goes to him and kneels beside him.*) What a dreamy boy! Look at him! (*He turns and smiles at her abstractedly.*) We're an odd pair, aren't we? Do you think it will be all right?

KENNETH. (*Abstractedly.*) Yes.

GINA. I can imagine what people will say . . . You won't mind?

KENNETH. No, no . . .

GINA. Perhaps it's all right. Perhaps it's just what you've been saying—we're so ill-matched that it *must* be all right!

KENNETH. Yes.

GINA. Oh, I'm so happy! Are you?

KENNETH. Yes.

GINA. What are you thinking about?

KENNETH. Oh, nothing.

GINA. You're not worrying about something? (*He sighs.*) You mustn't worry your head about anything now. That's all over.

KENNETH. I was just thinking.

GINA. Why don't you have a little rest from thinking?

KENNETH. I was just thinking about us, as the days go by, sitting here having breakfast together. You being all kind and motherly and sewing the buttons on my shirts. The house smelling all neat and quiet . . .

GINA. (*Smiling reflectively.*) I'm thinking about it too.

KENNETH. Well . . . there's going to be more to it than meets the eye, isn't there? What's going to be underneath it all?

GINA. You do want to come and live here?

KENNETH. Yes! But . . .

GINA. You are happy about it?

KENNETH. Yes, I'm *happy* . . .

GINA. *I'm* happy!

KENNETH. *I'm* happy! But . . .

GINA. But what?

KENNETH. But here we sit—we keep saying we're happy . . . What are we trying to hide from ourselves?

GINA. Are we trying to hide something from ourselves?

KENNETH. Gina, I explained it all!

GINA. But are you sure it works this way round as well?

KENNETH. Well, doesn't it? If you see somebody else leading what looks like a contented life, don't you immediately know that there are all sorts of hidden tensions and resentments underneath? (*She thinks.*)

GINA. Perhaps what we're trying to hide from ourselves is the fact that we actually *are* happy.

KENNETH. (*Doubtfully.*) Yes . . . But when I think of all that happiness, stretching on and on . . .

GINA. (*Cradling his head.*) Oh, love, you're so young! You expect so much! What you've got to do now is to grow up just a tiny bit, and learn another of life's little lessons. You've got to understand that when you've finally got what you want in this world, you don't want what you've got after all. It's really just what you were saying yourself, isn't it? Now, I'm going to tuck you up on the couch here . . . (*She does so.*) And you can have a nice little snooze before lunch.

KENNETH. Yes, but . . .

GINA. Sh! Don't worry your head about it any more! I'm going to put the joint on. Nice crispy brown potatoes —thick squelchy Yorkshire pudding! Think of that! (*She goes towards the stairs door, then turns back to him.*) Just try to see it the other way round: if you don't want what you've got, that proves you've got what you want!

KENNETH. (*Doubtfully.*) Yes . . . (*The he sees the attraction of the idea.*) Yes! (*And then he loses sight of it again.*) Yes . . . (*Fade to black.*)

MR. FOOT

CHARACTERS

GEOFFREY

NIBS

SETTING

Their living room.

MR. FOOT

Evening. GEOFFREY *and* NIBS *are sitting in armchairs, both reading solid-looking volumes. He has the air of a don, or senior civil servant, though he is in fact neither; she of a don's wife. For some time there is silence.* GEOFFREY *wrinkles his nose to slide his spectacles a little further up, and a few seconds later she does the some. Then one of his feet, crossed over the other knee, begins to jiggle impatiently. It continues for some moments, with unconscious mechanical persistence.* NIBS *lifts her head slightly and watches it. He feels her eye upon him. The foot stops jiggling and he looks up.*

GEOFFREY. What?

NIBS. Foot.

GEOFFREY. Ah. (*They both return to their books. After a few moments the foot starts to jiggle again, and* NIBS *looks up. He immediately stops, and uncrosses his legs. She continues to watch him, and after a few moments he looks up from his book and returns her gaze.*) What?

NIBS. This job . . .

GEOFFREY. What job?

NIBS. This job you're in line for . . .

GEOFFREY. What about it?

NIBS. You're *in line* for it?

GEOFFREY. (*Returning to his book.*) I'm *in line* for it, yes.

NIBS. What does that mean, precisely—*in line?*

GEOFFREY. (*After a pause, without looking up.*) *In line* means *in line.* That's what *in line* means.

NIBS. Ah.

GEOFFREY. (*Looking up sharply.*) What?

NIBS. Ah! (*He returns to his book. She continues to*

41

watch him. His foot jiggles briefly.) And am *I* on show this time?

GEOFFREY. (*After a pause, without looking up.*) The Chairman may want to *take a squint* at you. I don't know. This firm may not be in the habit of *taking a squint* at wives. On the other hand, it may. (*She stops looking at him, and gazes into space ahead of her. When she next speaks, it is directed primarily at herself.*)

NIBS. I suppose I shall wear the navy shantung, with a little pearl spray over the left breast . . . (*She holds out her hand, smiling.*) 'How very kind of you to ask us . . . ! What a beautiful part of the world! What a beautiful house! What lovely girls! what handsome boys!' (*She inclines her head back and to one side, with eyes closed, in a gesture of silent laughter.*) 'Does he? Really, the things we wives have to put up with! Do you know, up to a few years ago Geoffrey insisted on wearing his old army issue tropical shorts on the beach!' (*She turns to the person sitting on the other side of her, and thrusts her chin forward challengingly.*) 'Now tell me the truth, Sir Harold! Isn't your company doing exactly what all those wicked Spaniards did in the seventeenth century— plundering the New World to enrich the Old? Aren't you really the conquistadors of the modern age?' (GEOFFREY's *foot starts to jiggle. She smilingly offers her hand again.*) 'Well, that was a wonderful evening! Thank you so much! I always adore dinner-parties, because Geoffrey's foot is hidden under the table, and I can't see whether it's on the jig or not . . .' (*The foot abruptly stops jiggling.*)

GEOFFREY. (*Without looking up.*) Bear in mind that it may not be a dinner-party this time. They may send someone here. (*She stares at him. He looks up.*) It's a progressive company. They'll put a professional on the job, probably—send a *dick* round.

NIBS. A *dick?* To dinner?

GEOFFREY. No—to watch the house. See who goes in, who comes out. See how many *boy-friends* you've got.

(*They both resume their reading.* GEOFFREY *smiles to himself.*) Count the *boy-friends* going in the front. Count the empties coming out the back. *Sex* and *booze*—that's the sort of thing a progressive employer wants to know about. (NIBS *looks up and watches him coldly, as he smiles to himself.*) Then no doubt he'll come to the door. Take a *decko* at you from close to.

NIBS. I shan't let him in.

GEOFFREY. Of course you'll let him in.

NIBS. I most certainly shall not.

GEOFFREY. You won't know who it is. He'll be disguised as a brush salesman, or a market-research *johnny*.

NIBS. I don't let brush salesman in.

GEOFFREY. You'll let this one in, because these people are *professionally trained* to get into people's homes. Unless I am very much mistaken, you are not *professionally trained* to keep them out. (*His foot jiggles.*) Once inside, he'll no doubt start *banging off* questions.

NIBS. If he starts *banging off* questions I shall know he's not a brush salesman.

GEOFFREY. Not if they are questions about brushes!

NIBS. About brushes?

GEOFFREY. To begin with.

NIBS. 'How often do you sweep the floor?'

GEOFFREY. They will no doubt become more personal.

NIBS. 'Do you clean your teeth up and down or side to side?' (*His foot jiggles as he reads.*)

GEOFFREY. In any case, it won't be a brush salesman. It will be a market researcher. (*They both read for some moments. Then he looks up again.*) You won't have a chance to put your *fancy dress* on, you realise. (*He returns to his book. She slowly lifts her head and gazes at him expressionlessly.* GEOEFFREY'S *foot suffers a brief spasm of jiggling, but is brought under control. She returns to her book. He looks up again.*) What will you say to him? You'd better think of something before he arrives, hadn't you? Otherwise you'll get into one of your *muddles.* I shan't be here when he comes, of course. (*She slowly lifts her head.*)

NIBS. I shan't get into a muddle just because you're not here! It's you sitting there shaking your foot at me that gets me into my muddles.

GEOFFREY. You have your muddles with or without the assistance of my foot. My foot is neither here nor there. (*It jiggles briefly, and is brought under control.*) Not that it's anything to do with me, of course, whether you get into a muddle when this man calls.

NIBS. (*Sarcastically.*) No, if you don't get the job because I've had one of my muddles, that's nothing to do with you *at all.*

GEOFFREY. I leave it entirely to you. As long as you know what you are going to say . . .

NIBS. Oh, I shall say— (*To her imaginary interviewer.*) Sit down, sit down! Make yourself at him . . . !

GEOFFREY. You don't have to rehearse it to me! I'm not your form-mistress!

NIBS. No, I must get it right! We don't want one of my muddles!

GEOFFREY. Just run through it in your head, that's all I'm suggesting. You're not a child.

NIBS. No, no—I shall say— (*To interviewer.*) Do sit down! My word, you have an interesting job, going round talking to all these wives, seeing the way we live! Tell me, are we all going out of our minds with frustration and boredom, as everyone says . . . ? (*To* GOEFFREY.) Is this right? Am I doing it right?

GEOFFREY. It's not a question of *doing it right!* I wish you wouldn't keep asking me if you're *doing things right!* Just do what you think best! (GEOFFREY's *foot jiggles vigorously.* NIBS *turns back to the interviewer.*)

NIBS. Something I've always wanted to know—do any of the other wives you see have husbands with a foot problem? (*The foot stops abruptly.*)

GEOFFREY. I'm not listening.

NIBS. (*To interviewer.*) He's not listening. Nothing new

in that, of course. He never does. Which is why it's rather pleasant to have someone come to the house who is actually *paid* to listen. If I say something to Geoffrey, there's always a long pause, and then . . . (*A long pause. Then* GEOFFREY, *becoming at last aware that a sentence has been left hanging in the air, looks up.*)

GEOFFREY. (*Irritably.*) What?

NIBS. (*To interviewer.*) It's like being sick—it's the waiting for it to happen that's the worst part. Would you like a drink?

GEOFFREY. A drink? In the middle of the evening?

NIBS. (*To* GEOFFREY.) Not you. Him.

GEOFFREY. Him a drink? In the middle of the day? That won't create a very good impression.

NIBS. (*To interviewer.*) Whisky? Gin and something? A glass of beer perhaps? (*To* GEOFFREY.) It's not even the middle of the day! It's just after breakfast, if you want to know. I haven't made the beds yet! The house is in chaos! I'm not even *dressed!* (*To interviewer.*) Just throw that vacuum-cleaner off the chair if it's in your way! It's like a pig-sty in here anyway . . . A gin-and-tonic? Very good idea—I'll have one, too. If we really get down to it we can drink ourselves stupid before elevenses. (*She mimes pouring the drinks.* GEOFFREY, *who has been watching her with distaste, returns to his book.*)

GEOFFREY. I'm not listening to all this rubbish, you know.

NIBS. I should hope not! Mr. . . . (*She looks interrogatively at her interviewer.*) Samuelson, Mr. Samuelson. Mr. Samuelson and I are talking privately. Aren't we, Mr. Samuelson? What . . . ? Oh, cheers. (*She mimes raising her glass and drinking. To* GEOFFREY.) If Mr. Samuelson says 'cheers' I shall say 'cheers.' (*To Mr. Samuelson.*) Now, what do you want to know about me? Am I a suitable wife? Well, yes, I am, I'm an entirely suitable wife, thanks to the very thorough training that Geoffrey gave me in the early years of our marriage. 'Just be yourself,' he used to say, when we went out to dinner.

'Don't keep saying "Geoffrey says . . ." and "Geoffrey thinks . . ." Don't keep looking at me to see if I approve. Just behave naturally! But don't keep starting sentences that trail away into nothingness, and don't keep saying wild, meaningless things that end up in screams of laughter. If you can't think of anything sensible and natural to say, just smile quietly to yourself.' Of course, Geoffrey is largely retired from teaching now, but his able assistant Mr. Foot carries on the good work. (GEOFFREY's *foot jiggles, but is quickly brought under control.*) I lead a very full life. I read; I paint. And of course there's my *work* at the Citizens' Advice Bureau. Incidentally, I don't recall seeing you around when I applied for it, *taking a squint* at Geoffrey to see whether he was a suitable husband . . . ? I suppose you went round to his office, disguised as an insurance salesman . . . (*To* GEOFFREY.) Did anyone come to *take a squint* at *you* when *I* applied for *my* job? (*There is no reaction. She turns back reassuringly to Samuelson.*) Don't worry—we shall get a reply in two or three days at the very outside. What can we talk about in the meantime? You know we have two sons? Both away at university now. Do you have to check to see if *they're* suitable . . . ?

GEOFFREY. (*Looking up.*) What?

NIBS. (*To Samuelson.*) Ah, we're through. (*To* GEOFFREY.) Did anyone come to *take a squint* at *you* when *I* applied for *my* job?

GEOFFREY. Why should anyone want to *take a squint* at me?

NIBS. (*To Samuelson.*) What I can never understand is how and why he's managed to become so much like a Professor of Greek, when he's in fact a successful businessman. Let alone how he's managed to turn me into a professor's wife. (GEOFFREY's *foot jiggles.*)

GEOFFREY. If you're trying to *take a dig* at me you're wasting your breath. I've told you I'm not listening.

NIBS. Then why is Mr. Foot on the jig? (*It stops.*)

GEOFFREY. I wish you wouldn't call it Mr. Foot.

NIBS. (*To Samuelson.*) Mr. Foot thinks I'm giving you the wrong impression.

GEOFFREY. One of these days you'll start talking about Mr. Foot when there's someone around to hear.

NIBS. (*To SAMUELSON.*) We never mention Mr. Foot in public, you see.

GEOFFREY. You're working yourself up into one of your *muddles*. Why don't you either get quietly on with your book, or take some of those pills Dr. Farquhar gave you and go to bed? (*He returns to his book. NIBS sits watching him for a moment, apparently silenced. Then she turns discreetly back to Mr. Samuelson, and, glancing cautiously at her husband to see if he is listening, gestures with the imaginary bottle to Mr. Samuelson to let her recharge his glass. She pours some more for herself, conspiring with Mr. Samuelson aginst her husband. She smiles at him and silently raises her glass to him.*)

NIBS. (*In a low voice, to Samuelson.*) He doesn't like gin. He thinks it's only drunk by women, and men who join tennis clubs. (*She glances at* GEOFFREY *again. Her manner suggests that the whole conversation is behind* GEOFFREY'S *back.*) He won't eat anything fried, or anything frozen, or any fruit out of a tin, or any pudding out of a packet, or anything *pretending to be Italian* . . . I sit here for hours wondering what to give him for dinner . . . I sit painting my pictures . . . (*She mimes it.*) . . . and what am I thinking? I'm thinking— (*She speaks slowly and abstractedly, leaning forward to work on the detail of the picture.*) 'I wonder if *oeufs Florentine* are *pretending to be Italian?*' And then I think, 'Oh my God! He told me to ring the man about mending the fence before twelve . . . !' (*She glances anxiously at her watch, then hurriedly begins to put her brushes away, and get to her feet.*) 'I wonder if he caught his plane to Belfast all right . . . ?' (*She is just about to hurry away to the phone when another thought strikes her, and she stops, appalled.*) 'I did put the flask of coffee in his brief-

case, didn't I? If he has to drink BEA coffee there and
back he'll come home this evening in a great state of
silent moral outrage. He'll sit there reading "Coins of the
Greek Colonies in Italy," and Mr. Foot will go jig-jig-jig-
jig-jig . . . (*Mr. Foot does so, but* GEOFFREY *seizes it and
holds it.*) 'What's the matter?' 'What? Nothing's the
matter.' But Mr. Foot thinks something's the matter.
Disagrees with some statement in the book, perhaps. No,
something I've done. I haven't wound the hall clock again
. . . I've forgotten to put any stockings on . . . I've put
the newpapers under the cushions . . . I've left the
lavatory light on all day . . . (*She sits down again,
watching* GEOFFREY *apprehensively.*) 'Had a good
day?'— No, no, no, that's wrong! Strike that out of the
record! He thinks that's suburban—something we certainly can't afford to be, living as we do in the suburbs.
Let's see . . . 'How was Belfast, then?' No, no, no! I
asked that about Amsterdam last week. 'How was Amsterdam?' 'What?' 'How was Amsterdam?' Jig-jig-jig-jig-
jig! 'I'm afraid I didn't inquire after its health.' *'Sorry!*
Now . . . I know: 'Did you catch the plane all right?'
(*Pause.*) 'What?' 'Did you catch the plane all right?'
'Yes.' (*Pause.*) 'Let's think, what can I ask him now? We
can't have reached the end of our conversational resources
already. 'Did you catch the plane *back* all right?'
(*Pause.*) 'What?—Yes.' All right so far! But what's this?
Mr. Foot's on the go! I've bored Mr. Foot! Said too
much! Said something vulgar! You'd never believe how
easy it is to upset Mr. Foot! If Mr. Foot could hear what
I'm telling you now he'd have to be held down! (GEOFFREY
*at once lets go of the foot. In an instant it starts to jiggle
again. He seizes it once more. She pours Mr. Samuelson
and herself more drinks.*) Mr. Foot would think I was
representing myself as *the little woman* just to annoy
him. Mr. Foot doesn't like me to be *the little woman!* The
medium-sized woman, yes; but not the little one . . .
Cheers . . . ! Woo, I'm starting to feel rather dizzy . . . !
So let me assure you, just in case he can overhear us, just

in case he's got the place bugged—oh, I wouldn't put it
past him!—no I wouldn't!—oh, he's as mad as a
hatter!— (*Into an imaginary microphone.*) Yes, cooee,
can you hear me? We're talking about you! (*To Samuelson.*) —Let me assure you I get my own back! For
instance, I put frozen beans in the goulash! He never
notices. (*Into the microphone.*) Do you hear that? Frozen
beans in the goulash! (*To Samuelson.*) Though why food
pretending to be Hungarian is permitted I cannot imagine
. . . What else do I do? Well, I wrap the rubbish in the
morning papers by mistake. I have one of my *muddles*
and I forget to buy stockings, so that I have to go to
the Traffords with bare legs. Yes, to the Traffords! Twice
now! With absolutely nothing whatsoever around the
lower legs! Just naked white skin! And when we get
there, what happens? I feel another of my muddles coming on! I start every sentence with 'Geoffrey thinks . . .',
'Geoffrey says . . .', 'According to Geoffrey . . .' And I
finish every sentence with '. . . don't you, Geoffrey?'
'. . . have I got that right, Geoffrey?' And Mr. Foot's
hidden under the table, so I never know what he thinks
at all, except at the Costains, where they've got a table
with wobbly legs, and I can feel the whole thing shaking
with disapproval. (*The imaginary table she is sitting at
shakes beneath her hands. At the same moment* GEOF-
FREY'S *foot breaks loose and jiggles. He seizes his foot.
She seizes the table.*) It's this *ménage à trois* with his
friend Mr. Foot which is so difficult to bear. (*She re-
charges Mr. Samuelson's glass and her own.*) I wonder
what *Foot* does at the office all day. That's what I'd like
to know . . . I don't know what I'm saying; I'm a little
bit drunk. You'll be running away with the idea that I'm
jealous of my husband's foot! It's not jealousy—it's just
that I think it's getting a hold *over* him . . . which I
don't think it's right for a foot to have over a man . . .
(*She catches sight of it, and gives a little wave and forced
smile.*) Hello! (*To Samuelson.*) It's watching us. (*To
foot, offering bottle.*) Like a drink? (*To Samuelson, as*

she extends the bottle towards the foot, as if about to pour it a drink.) I'll get it drunk. Then it might tell us a thing or two. (*The foot jiggles briefly.*) No? (*She turns back to Samuelson.*) It's got such a negative attitude to life, that's what I dislike so much. All it can do is disapprove! I think a healthy, normal foot would try to encourage you, as well—give you a pat on the back from time to time. Don't you? (*The foot jiggles briefly.*) Don't take any notice of it. No, no—don't look at it. We must make plans. We'll wait till it's asleep, then overpower it. We'll put a sack over its head—tie it up—drag it to the river and throw it in. Then we'll go away. Yes, we'll run away together! We'll start a new life! We'll go to Canada —I have friends there. I'll go out to work—we won't starve . . . (GEOFFREY *lifts his eyes from his book and gazes at her.*) He's listening! I told you—the whole place is bugged! (*She meets his disquieted gaze. They stare at each other in silence for a moment. Then she turns back to Samuelson.*) He heard everything! He's thinking out what to say! Whether to be outraged, or understanding . . . ! (*She meets* GEOFFREY'S *gaze again. A pause.*)

GEOFFREY. What's that smell? Did you leave something on the stove?

NIBS. (*To Samuelson.*) Did I leave something on the stove!

GEOFFREY. What?

NIBS. (*To* GEOFFREY.) No, I didn't leave anything on the stove! It's the boiler smelling again.

GEOFFREY. Ah. (*He returns to his book.*)

NIBS. Have you been listening to what I was saying? (*A pause.*)

GEOFFREY. What?

NIBS. Have you been listening?

GEOFFREY. You know I never listen when you're having one of your *muddles.* I just leave you to get on with it in peace and work it out of your system.

NIBS. (*To Samuelson.*) He hasn't been listening. It's Foot who listens, of course. Foot listens, and from time to

time submits reports on the situation to headquarters.
That's what all that jiggling is—it's Foot tapping out his
reports in Morse. They don't take it very seriously up at
headquarters. Old Nibs is having one of her muddles
again, they think. (Nibs is me; I'm called Nibs. Did you
know that? Unbelievable, isn't it? How did *that* happen?)
Old Nibs is holding another demonstration for women's
rights—old Nibs is marching up and down outside again
with banners and slogans. Well, that's all right—it'll keep
her out of mischief; that's what Geoffrey thinks. (Here
we go again—'Geoffrey thinks . . .'—'Geoffrey says . . .'!)
Geoffrey thinks I get into my muddles just to irritate
him. Well, certainly I do! Undoubtedly! But supposing
one day I get into one of my muddles and I can't get out
again! They'll cart me off to the muddlehouse! Think
how Foot will shake and dance and tap when *that*
happens! (*The foot suffers a spasm of jiggling.*) There
he goes, just at the thought of it! Geoffrey will think
I've got myself put in the muddlehouse just to annoy
him! And that might be true! That's what he can't stand,
you see—the thought that I don't have any existence
independent of him, that everything I do is just to please
or annoy him. 'Just be yourself!' he used to say, when he
still had hopes. 'Don't look at me all the time to see if I
approve!' He wants me to be *his*. But of course I can't be
his unless I'm separate from him—unless I remain *me*.
He's like a little child with a soap-bubble; he can't enjoy
it unless he can hold it, and as soon as he tries to hold it
it vanishes. He thinks I've become just another part of
himself! And a nagging, troublesome part at that! A tooth
with the toothache! Another foot with the shakes! And
of course he feels it reflects badly on him, having to admit
to the world that he's married to his foot. 'You've met
my left and right feet, but I don't think you've met my
foot Nibs, have you?' (*Confidentially.*) 'She goes on the
twitch from time to time. Don't pay any attention. It's
just a slight disability I suffer from.' Well, he's going to
get a surprise when he looks up from his book one day

and discovers that I've run off with you to Canada!
'What? Run away with the *dick* who was sent to check
that she was a suitable wife? What will the bloke put
in his report now?' But he'd be even more surprised if
he knew what I was thinking and talking about over there
in Canada! Because it wouldn't be about him! Oh no! I
shouldn't be saying, 'Geoffrey thinks . . .' and 'Geoffrey
says . . .' all the time. I'd be myself! I'd be running
through the forests with bare legs, living off frozen peas
and tinned pears and spaghetti bolognaise out of a
packet! And leaving all the lights on! And putting all
the newspapers under the cushions! I'd just be laughing
and laughing and laughing . . . (*She laughs at the
thought of it.*) . . . and saying, 'how surprised Geoffrey
would be, if only he could see me now . . . !' (*The
elation drains out of her, as she realises what she is
saying.*) '. . . for once not even thinking about him.'
(*A silence. She sits gazing in absent-minded dejection at
his foot. Gradually the absence of sound makes him first
jiggle the foot, then look up.*)

GEOFFREY. What? (*She doesn't respond.*) All over,
then? Why don't you *toddle along?* Get a good night's
rest in case this bloke comes? (*Still no response.*) Don't
want to find yourself getting in one of your muddles
with *him.* (GEOFFREY *returns to his book.* NIBS *sighs,
and gets up as if to go. She catches sight of his foot, and
kneels down in front of it.*)

NIBS. (*To the foot.*) Well, then, *you* tell him. He'll
listen to you. Just explain what the situation is, that's all.
Just tell him—oh, I don't know—tell him . . . (*The
foot jiggles violently. She moves back, discouraged.*) Tell
him to lock up before he comes to bed. (*She gets to her
feet and turns to go. Curtain.*)

CHINAMEN

CHARACTERS

STEPHEN
BARNEY } *The actor*

JO
BEE } *The actress*
ALEX

SETTING

The dining-room of Stephen and Jo's house, with the
table laid for six. There are three doors leading off—one
into the kitchen, one into the living-room, and the third
into a corridor which gives access to lavatory, stairs, back
door, etc. There is also a window overlooking the street.
It is dark outside.

CHINAMEN

Jo *enters hurriedly through the corridor door, still strug-*
gling into her dress. She begins to check the dinner
table, balancing on one evening shoe and counting
the cutlery with the other.

Jo. (*At speed.*) Knife knife fork fork spoon, knife
knife fork fork spoon, knife knife fork fork spoon . . .
Soup spoons! Oh, my God! (*She hobbles hurriedly out to*
the kitchen, holding her unzipped dress up.)
   GIRL CHILD. (*Off.*) Mummy, can we come down and
just say hello to all the people? (Jo *at once comes out of*
the kitchen, shouting in the direction of the corridor
door.)
   Jo. No! Go to sleep, both of you! (*She shuts the cor-*
ridor door firmly and hurries back into the kitchen. As
she does so, STEPHEN *hurries in from the living-room,*
carrying another dining-chair to add to the four around
the table.)
   STEPHEN. It's ten past eight, Jo!
   Jo. Don't tell *me* it's ten past eight! (*He puts the chair*
down and heads back at once towards the living-room.)
   STEPHEN. John and whatsit aways arrive at eight-
fifteen sharp for eight o'clock. Oh God, I've forgotten her
name again! (*He goes out into the living-room.* Jo *re-*
emerges from the kitchen, carrying soup spoons.)
   Jo. *Laura* . . . / It's getting the children to bed that
does it—we'll *have* to get another *au pair*, Stephen . . .
Oh, not that one—that's the one with the dicky leg. (*She*
picks up the chair which STEPHEN *has just brought in,*
and hurries it out to the kitchen, still holding spoons,
shoe, and dress. As she does so, STEPHEN *hurries back in*
from the living-room carrying another chair.)

55

STEPHEN. Laura, Laura, Laura . . . My block about names gets worse and worse every day!

Jo. Get another chair out of the living-room, Stephen. I'm putting the dicky one in the kitchen so no one can sit on it by mistake. (*She goes out.*)

STEPHEN. (*Putting down the chair he is carrying, and heading back for another.*) David and *Laura!* David and *Laura!* David and *Laura . . .* ! (*He goes out into the living-room as* Jo *returns from the kitchen.*)

Jo. *John* and Laura! *John* and Laura! For heaven's sake get it straight, Stephen. We've known them for ten years! (*She starts hurriedly distributing soup spoons, as* STEPHEN *hurries back in with another chair.*)

STEPHEN. I can't really tell our friends apart, that's the trouble. John and Laura, John and Laura, John and Laura . . . They're all exactly the same—same age, same number of children, same sort of job, same income, same opinions. . . .

Jo. (*Surveying table.*) Zip me up, will you?

STEPHEN. (*Zipping her.*) They even look alike! It's like looking at Chinamen. Nicholas and Jay—Simon and Kay—Freddie and Di . . .

Jo. No doubt they think the same about us. Have you put the ice out for the drinks?

STEPHEN. Yes . . . Good God, *we're* not like that! Are we?

Jo. Now, John can sit at the head of the table . . .

STEPHEN. John and Laura, John and Laura, John and Laura . . .

Jo. Then Laura can sit *here* . . .

STEPHEN. (*Indicating.*) Bee next to John. John and Laura, John and Laura . . . Barney over there. At least I won't forget *their* names! Barney and Bee, my God!

Jo. (*Gazing at him, appalled.*) Not Barney and Bee, Stephen!

STEPHEN. What do you mean, not Barney and Bee? Of course it's Barney and Bee!

Jo. Stephen!

STEPHEN. Barney and Bee! Barney and Bee! I might forget David and Dora, but *Barney and Bee* . . . !

Jo. Stephen, she's left him! Bee's left Barney!

STEPHEN. No!

Jo. I *told* you!

STEPHEN. I don't remember that.

Jo. She couldn't stand it any longer! She just quietly left, without any fuss, about a week ago, and went off with a man called Alex!

STEPHEN. (*Rubbing his chin and struggling to focus his mind.*) Oh . . . Some faint memory does stir. A singer, or something, wasn't he?

Jo. He runs one of those psychedelic discotheque places.

STEPHEN. So it's not Barney and Bee any more?

Jo. No, darling. Alex and Bee.

STEPHEN. Alex and Bee. It doesn't sound very convincing somehow, does it?

Jo. Well, that's what it is. You won't forget again, will you, Stephen?

STEPHEN. Alex and Bee . . . Alex and Bee . . . Thank God you told me! So Barney'll be coming on his own tonight?

Jo. No, no, no—it's not Barney who's coming! It's Bee, and she's bringing Alex, so that we can meet him. Oh God—no napkins! (*She runs out to the kitchen to fetch them. He stands gazing after her, the ramifications of the situation slowly dawning on him.*)

STEPHEN. (*Appalled.*) Alex and Bee are coming here tonight?

Jo. (*Running back in with the napkins.*) Yes, *Alex* and *Bee.* Do get it straight, darling. (*She rapidly distributes the napkins as* STEPHEN *gazes at her.*) Well, at least Alex will make a change from all the Chinamen. According to Sara Dolomore he's about nineteen, with hair down to his shoulders, and strings of beads, and dingle-dangles all over him . . . What are you looking like that for, Stephen?

STEPHEN. Jo, I've done a terrible thing!

Jo. What do you mean?

STEPHEN. Well, I ran into Barney at lunchtime today. I'd entirely forgotten about Bee leaving him . . .

Jo. (*Despairingly.*) So you asked after her? You said, 'And how is your very lovely wife?'

STEPHEN. No. I said, 'See you this evening, then.'

Jo. Stephen, you didn't!

STEPHEN. And he said, 'This evening? What do you mean?' And I said, ' You're coming to dinner this evening!'

Jo. And he said, 'No, I'm not—you must have mixed me up with Simon, or Mark, or Nicholas.' I bet you felt a fool!

STEPHEN. No, he said, 'Thanks, Stephen. You don't know how much that means to me just at the moment.' I thought at the time it was a slightly odd thing to say.

Jo. Oh, my God!

STEPHEN. Anyway, so I said, 'Eight o'clock, then!' And he said, 'Eight o'clock!' (*They both look at their watches, and then stare at each other.*)

Jo. (*Wildly.*) Well, ring him up! Stop him!

STEPHEN. It's no good ringing him at quarter past eight! He'll be on his way—he's probably on the doorstep now!

Jo. What a bloody stupid thing to do!

STEPHEN. Bloody stupid thing inviting your lot, if it comes to that! Fancy inviting Bee without Barney and not telling me!

Jo. I did tell you! You just weren't listening, you stupid oaf!

STEPHEN. Well, fancy not making sure I was listening! Anyway, I *was* listening. I wasn't remembering, that's all.

Jo. You weren't remembering!

STEPHEN. Oh, for heaven's sake don't waste time arguing!

Jo. I'm not the one who's wasting time . . . !

STEPHEN. (*Shouting.*) All right, then! So let's decide

what we're going to do before . . . (*The front door bell rings. They gaze at each other.*)

Jo. Don't let them in!

STEPHEN. We've got to let them in! Anyway, that'll be David and whatsit, David and Nora.

Jo. John and Laura. (*As she speaks she goes to the window and tries to see them through the crack in the curtains.*) But we mustn't let *anyone* in till we've thought out what we're going to do.

STEPHEN. Oh, for heaven's sake! They'll all be meeting on the doorstep!

Jo. Well, at least if they meet on the doorstep we shan't have to watch.

STEPHEN. Perhaps the first thing is to decide exactly what we're trying to do. Why are we so frightened of them meeting? Are we trying to spare their feelings, or is it just our own embarrassment that we're worried about?

Jo. I've a good mind to walk out the back door and leave you to get on with it.

STEPHEN. My God! If anyone should be walking out it's me! I mean, let's reason this out one step at a time . . . (*The bell rings again. They stare at each other, undecided. Then* STEPHEN *gives in.*) Oh . . . ! (*He hurries out through the living-room.* Jo *rushes to the window for another look through the crack in the curtains, then runs to the mirror and has a last quick look at herself. Then she goes to the living-room door and opens it a crack, listening to hear who it is.*)

STEPHEN. (*Jovially, off.*) . . . no, no, no, not late at all. Just right. Come in and sit yourselves down . . . (*She shuts the door, hurries to the table, and distractedly dabs at the cutlery.* STEPHEN *reappears from the living-room, still speaking to* JOHN *and* LAURA *as he turns to shut the door.*) Excuse me a moment. One or two little . . . you know . . . (*He nods jovially to complete the sense, then shuts the door and turns tensely to face* Jo.) David and Dora . . .

Jo. John and Laura.

STEPHEN. What are we going to do? (*He opens the door again and calls jovially off to* JOHN *and* LAURA.) Fix yourselves drinks, will you, um . . . ?

Jo. John.

STEPHEN. John. (*He shuts the door and turns back to* Jo.) We must have a clear and definite plan of campaign. (*He opens the door and continues jovially to* JOHN *and* LAURA.) Over there! On the side! Right . . . (*He shuts the door and turns back to* Jo.) We can't just stand here and wait for it to happen.

Jo. No, well, look . . . (*She beckons him urgently over to the window to show him what she has in mind.*) You go down and wait outside the front door, and when Barney arrives, get rid of him.

STEPHEN. Get rid of him? How?

Jo. I don't know. Make something up. Tell him the children are infectious—tell him the pipes have burst. Tell him the truth, why not? We've known him for long enough. He'll see the funny side of it.

STEPHEN. 'Barney, a rather amusing mistake has occurred! We didn't really mean to invite *you* at all—it was your wife and her new boy friend we meant . . . !'

Jo. (*Bundling him towards the living-room door.*) Tell him something else, then.

STEPHEN. He's going to be terribly hurt whatever I tell him. He was setting so much store by this.

Jo. If the worst comes to the worst, take him out to a restaurant, and I'll tell the others you've been called away on business . . . (*Still extremely reluctant, he allows himself to be bundled through the living-room door. As it opens they both compose their faces for their guests.*)

STEPHEN. (*Jovially, to* JOHN *and* LAURA.) Got drinks, then? Good, good, good. Sit down and relax—I'm just passing through . . . (*He disappears.*)

Jo. Hello! Hello! No, don't get up! I'm just putting my head round the door! I've got one or two . . . you know . . . (*She gestures vaguely behind her.*) In the

kitchen . . . and the children . . . terrible muddle . . .
completely disorganised, I'm afraid . . . ! Anyway, I'm
glad you managed to get here all right . . . (*She smiles
reassuringly, and shuts the door. Then she runs to the
window, draws the curtains back, and looks out. She opens
the window, calls to* STEPHEN *in a stage whisper, enun-
ciating carefully.*) Stephen! If Alex and Bee arrive first,
I'll let them in. *You* hide behind the dustbins, and wait
for Barney. (*She draws the curtains again and goes back
to the living-room to address a few more words to her
guests.*) All right still? Good. You will keep helping yourselves to drinks, won't you? Oh, that reminds me . . .
(*She shuts the living-room door and hurries back to the
window. She draws the curtains back and calls to*
STEPHEN.) Have you got any money on you, if you have
to take Barney out . . . ? *Money* . . . ! Hold on, then
. . . (*She hurries back to the living-room and opens the
door.*) How are you both these days? I don't think I ever
asked you . . . (*She makes a brief foray into the living-
room as she says this, and continues without pause as she
emerges holding her handbag.*) *Do* pour yourselves another drink—I've got to pay the milkman . . . (*She
shuts the door and returns to the window, where she
throws the money out to* STEPHEN.) Here you are. Five
pounds, all I've got . . . (*The corridor door opens, and*
BARNEY *looks in. Jo is still leaning out of the window.*)
But don't take him if you can possibly get shot of him by
any other . . .

BARNEY. (*Tapping with belated discretion on the
door.*) Anyone at home? (JO *spins guiltily around, drawing the curtains behind her.*)

Jo. Barney!

BARNEY. I came the back way, I hope you don't mind.
There's some rather thuggish-looking customer lurking
about on your front doorstep. Drug-addict, probably,
looking for money. (*He kisses her.*)

Jo. (*Confused.*) Barney, I was just going to . . . We
were just thinking . . .

BARNEY. I hope I'm not too late. (*He hands her his briefcase and umbrella.*) Been sitting in the pub ever since six o'clock. Couldn't face going home to an empty house. Just waiting for the moment to come round here. Then when the time came . . . I thought I'd just have another drink first. You know how it is, when you're just killing time.

Jo. Barney, there's something I've got to tell you right away, before you come in . . .

BARNEY. Thanks, Jo—but let's not even talk about it. I know how you feel.

Jo. I'm terribly sorry about Bee leaving you, Barney. I really am. Look, I don't quite know how to put this, but . . .

BARNEY. I know—you just don't know what to say to someone when something like this happens, do you? I don't know what to say about it myself. Ten years, and then—woof! It's quite a shock.

Jo. Yes. But the thing is, Barney . . .

BARNEY. She's gone off with a pouf. Or so I gather. Did you know that? I'm told he wears ear-rings—got hair halfway down his back. I mean how does that make me look? It makes me a complete laughing-stock, doesn't it?

Jo. Yes, but listen, Barney . . .

BARNEY. I haven't so far had the pleasure of making his acquaintance. I'm about the only person in town who hasn't, I may say. Do you know what she's done? She's wheeled him round to meet all our old friends, to get them all on her side! Wherever I go I find people have just had them to dinner! Then when I turn up they're embarrassed. They don't want to know me. People who have been friends for years!

Jo. Barney . . .

BARNEY. I mean, I take it you haven't just . . .

Jo. No, no, no. But . . .

BARNEY. It's always the same when a couple splits up. No one wants to take sides, but everyone does.

Jo. Yes, but . . .

Barney. I was just going to say, that's why I'm so very touched to be invited here tonight . . . Sorry, you were going to say something. (*She looks at him as if she is, then changes her mind.*)

Jo. No, no. Just that . . . it's very nice to see you.

Barney. (*Putting his arm round her, and leading her towards the living-room.*) Bless you, Jo. You really find out who your friends are when something like this happens. Where's Stephen? In here?

Jo. (*Stopping short.*) Oh, my God, I'd forgotten all about him! He's just . . . fixing something outside. I'd better give him a call. (*She leads* Barney *firmly towards the kitchen.*) Now why don't you sit down quietly in the kitchen for a moment? Then we can have a little chat about things together while I'm getting the dinner.

Barney. (*Turning at the kitchen door.*) Jo, you're a real brick. You and Stephen—don't you ever . . .

Jo. No, no.

Barney. I mean, old Stephen's like me. He may not seem very exciting, and so on, but . . .

Jo. Don't worry, Barney.

Barney. You're still . . . ? (*He links his little fingers together and pulls, in a gesture indicating solid attachment.*)

Jo. Yes.

Barney. (*Patting her on the shoulder.*) Good girl. (*She at last manages to get the door shut on him, and at once hurries across to the window. Just as she is drawing the curtains back,* Barney *puts his head out from the kitchen again.*)

Barney. (*Wagging his finger.*) I'm serious about that, Jo.

Jo. (*Whirling round to face* Barney.) Yes. Stay there, Barney. I'll bring you a drink. (*He goes back into the kitchen, leaving the door open. Jo opens the curtains with great precaution, and, glancing anxiously over her shoul-*

der at the open kitchen door, mouths silently to STEPHEN.) Barney's here! Come back! (*She pantomimes desperately, pointing at the kitchen and indicating that he should return. At last, evidently satisfied that he has understood, she closes the curtains and goes to the kitchen.*) What would you like—whisky? (*She hurries to the living-room, addressing* JOHN *and* LAURA *as she dives briefly in and emerges again holding up a bottle of whisky.*) How's Midge enjoying school . . . ? Need a drop of whisky for the soup—there's another bottle on the side. Do keep helping yourselves. (*She shuts the living-room door and hurries to the kitchen, where she hands the bottle through the open door to an arm which emerges to take it.*) Fix it yourself, will you, Barney? There's ice in the fridge . . . (*Having taken the bottle, the arm takes her hand, drawing it off, evidently to* BARNEY'S *lips. There is the sound of a kiss.*) Oh, Barney! (*She flutters her eyelashes, in hurried appreciation.*) Anyway, make yourself at home. I've just got to . . . you know . . . this and that . . . (*She shuts the kitchen door. As she does so, the living-room door opens and* STEPHEN *enters, talking jovially to* JOHN *and* LAURA.)

STEPHEN. That's right! Ships that pass in the night! Anyway, pour yourselves another drink . . . (*He closes the door and turns to face* Jo.) What is it?

Jo. He's here! Barney! He came in round the back.

STEPHEN. Oh, my God!

Jo. I've put him in the kitchen.

STEPHEN. In the kitchen?

Jo. In case Alex and Bee arrived before I could warn you.

STEPHEN. (*Irritated.*) You should have got rid of him. (*He goes to the kitchen, turning instantly jovial as he opens the door.*)

STEPHEN. Hello! Barney! Nice to see you!

BARNEY. (*Off.*) Stephen!

STEPHEN. (*Emerging again, still holding* BARNEY'S

hand.) Don't get up! Stay where you are! Got something to keep you occupied, have you? Anyway, pour yourself a drink. Oh, you have. That's the spirit! (*He smilingly disengages himself, shuts the door, and turns furiously upon* Jo.) Why didn't you get rid of him?

Jo. Oh, Stephen, I couldn't! He kept thanking me for inviting him—he thinks we're the only friends he's got left. He made me feel such a heel for inviting Alex and Bee.

STEPHEN. Oh, for God's sake! We can't start being sentimental at this stage!

Jo. (*With asperity.*) Well, *you* get rid of him!

STEPHEN. I can't get rid of him *now!* Now you've set him up in the kitchen with a bottle of Scotch!

Jo. Well, we'll just have to get rid of Alex and Bee instead.

STEPHEN. How?

Jo. I suppose you'll have to go down and wait outside the front door again. (STEPHEN *compresses his lips with reluctance.*)

STEPHEN. Supposing they come round the back, like Barney?

Jo. (*Pushing him towards the living-room door.*) Keep an eye on the back as well! Patrol back and forth! Good heavens, you were in the army—you know how to guard things. (*But just as he is about to open the living-room door, he rebels.*)

STEPHEN. Look, I can't just walk straight past David and Nora *again!*

Jo. John and Laura. Well, go out the back way, then! (Jo *urges* STEPHEN *towards the corridor door.*) Just get out there fast, that's all that matters, because any moment now they're going to be ringing that . . . (*The front door bell rings.* STEPHEN *and* Jo, *already holding the corridor door open, freeze. They gaze at each other in silence for a moment.*)

STEPHEN. *Now* what are we going to do?

Jo. Well, we'll just have to . . . I don't know . . . shout at them out of the window.

STEPHEN. Shout at them out of the window?

Jo. Explain what the situation is. Tell them to go away.

STEPHEN. Go on, then. (Jo *crosses to the window, and looks out through the crack in the curtain, irresolute. She makes as if to shout, but gives up.*)

Jo. Or we could just pretend not to be here. How about that? (*The bell rings again. As they stand undecided, the kitchen door begins to open. They notice it at once.*) Barney!

STEPHEN. (*Hurrying to bundle* BARNEY *back into the kitchen.*) Sit down, Barney! Have another drink! (*He goes into the kitchen, while* Jo *hovers anxiously at the door.*)

BARNEY. (*Off.*) I just thought you might like me to answer the bell, Stephen.

Jo. No, no, no, no!

STEPHEN. (*Re-emerging.*) No, no, no, no!

Jo. Just sit down and relax!

STEPHEN. We'll be out there to chat in a minute. (*They close the kitchen door, and look at each other. The front door bell rings again.*)

Jo. You'll *have* to answer it. Just open the door and send them away. (*She urges him towards the living-room.*) Just open the door, and explain everything quietly to them in the hall. They're reasonable people—they'll understand. Well, Bee's a reasonable person. She'll understand.

STEPHEN. (*Hesitating, his hand on the door handle.*) Bee? She's one of the least reasonable people I've ever come across.

Jo. Well, whatever you tell them, do it quickly, before they've got their coats off. (*With the utmost reluctance* STEPHEN *opens the door, switching on his jovial manner as he does so.*)

STEPHEN. Here I am again then! (*His face falls.*) Bee!

(*He turns to exchange one brief horror-stricken glance with* Jo.) They're in! (*He at once turns back towards his guests, reassembling has face even as his head turns.*) Bee, how lovely to see you! And this must be Alex! (STEPHEN *advances into the living-room.* Jo *closes the door behind him, in a state of shock.*)

Jo. Oh, my *Gawd!* (*At once the living-room door re-opens, and* STEPHEN *emerges, smiling jovially back at* ALEX *and* BEE.)

STEPHEN. Well, sit down! Make yourselves at home! (*He shuts the door, and turns haggardly to* Jo.) Dick and Dora let them in!

Jo. John and Laura.

STEPHEN. They've got their coats off! They're sitting down making themselves at home already! (*He opens the door and calls jovially into the room.*) Pour them drinks, will you, um . . . ?

Jo. John.

STEPHEN. John. (*He shuts the door.*) You were quite right about that Alex man. I've never seen anything like it—I can't imagaine what Bee was thinking of. Well, what are we going to do? We can't go and chuck them out now they're sitting down with drinks in their hands, talking to Thingummy and Whatsit, can we?

Jo. No. Well, I suppose they'll all three of them just have to be very adult and mature about it and face facts.

STEPHEN. You mean, face each other?

Jo. Well, there's nothing else for it, is there?

STEPHEN. This Alex lad doesn't look very adult or mature to me. I don't think his voice has broken yet.

Jo. Well, Barney and Bee will just have to be adult and mature about it.

STEPHEN. Bee's got her funny tense look on. At the slightest provocation she's going to burst into tears, or start playing Truth or Dare.

Jo. We'll have to tell them Barney's here, Stephen. There's no other way out of it.

STEPHEN. Well, I refuse. Point blank.

Jo. I'll do it, then.

STEPHEN. All right. (*Jo goes to the door and stands for a moment, thinking what she is going to say, trying out various social faces. Then she turns briefly back to* STEPHEN, *who is watching her anxiously.*)

Jo. You go and prepare Barney. (*Then she turns back to the door, puts on her social face, and at once throws the door open.*) Bee! How lovely to see you! *Super* dress . . . ! (*She advances into the room, closing the door behind her.* STEPHEN *grimaces after her, then reluctantly addresses himself to the job in the kitchen. He hesitates outside the kitchen door, thinking how he's going to broach the subject, then flings it open with determination and a jovial smile.*)

STEPHEN. How are you doing out here? Plenty to drink? Good . . . Er . . . (*He holds a sustained middle er, as if trying to remember what he is going to do next. Then, as if he has remembered and discovered that it lies elsewhere, he concludes the er with a brisk ah, and shuts the door. He has another think, drumming his fingertips on his front teeth, then resolutely flings open the door again. He repeats the sustained er, exactly as before, then notices* BARNEY'S *briefcase and umbrella. He hands them into the kitchen, as if this had been his intention all the time.*) Your stuff! (*He shuts the door. As he does so, the living-room door opens, and* Jo *comes out, laughing, and still talking to the occupants of the room.*)

Jo. . . . Of course not! I've been wanting to meet Alex for—oh, a week now! Pour yourselves another drink . . . (*She closes the door and turns to face* STEPHEN.)

STEPHEN. Well, what did they say?

Jo. (*Gloomily.*) I didn't tell them. What did Barney say?

STEPHEN. I didn't tell him.

Jo. It would have been one thing if Barney had just happened to be in the room when they'd come in. But you can't just say brightly in the middle of the conversation, 'Oh, by the way, we've got your husband out in the kitchen!'

STEPHEN. That was where it all went wrong, putting Barney in the kitchen.

Jo. It just doesn't seem natural. It's either got to happen naturally or not at all.

STEPHEN. It was your fault, putting him in the kitchen. I can't think what you were up to.

Jo. It seemed perfectly logical at the time.

STEPHEN. Anyway . . .

Jo. Anyway, we'll just have to find another way of doing it. We'll have to feed them separately, that's what it comes down to. We'll serve all this lot dinner in the living-room, and we'll give Barney his dinner in the kitchen. I think that's the answer, isn't it? (*She hurries to the dinner-table, and sets to work to off-load one complete place-setting on to a tray.*)

STEPHEN. But just a moment. Where will *we* have dinner—you and I? With Barney, or with the other lot?

Jo. Well . . . we'll rush back and forth between the two.

STEPHEN. They'll think that's a bit odd, won't they?

Jo. I don't see why. The host and hostess are always rushing in and out at dinner-parties. I'll run backwards and forwards with the food. You run backwards and forwards with the wine. (Jo *hands* STEPHEN *the loaded tray.*) There, that's for Barney. We'll be one short in there, but I don't suppose I'll have time to sit down, anyway. Now, just give me a hand with this table . . . (*He puts the tray aside, and helps her carry the table to the living-room door.*) Oh, come on! Don't look so doom-laden about it! We've had awkward situations at dinner-parties before, haven't we? If you give a dinner-party you expect something like this to happen! We'll cope! It's always been all right before!

STEPHEN. I sometimes wonder if life is worth living. (*He opens the door and backs into the living-room, addressing the occupants jovially.*) Here we are, then!

Meals on wheels! (*He disappears from view. The table is edged slowly through the door.*)

Jo. I thought it would make a change to eat out here for once! It gets such a bore, always using the dining-room for dining, and the living-room for living . . . (*Further progress is halted by some obstacle off, so just* Jo *remains on stage holding her end of the table, edging it up and down and back and forth as she speaks.*) Mind the lamp, darling! John, would you move that china albatross thing before Stephen . . . (*There is a crash of breaking china.*) Never mind! I always hated it! Just kick the bits under the sofa . . . Darling, we can't stand here all night . . . ! Well, lift you end *over* John's head . . . (*The offstage end of the table goes up, so that everything on it begins to slide towards* Jo. *She desperately raises her end.*) Down! Your end down! (*The offstage end goes down, so that everything slides the other way. She lowers her end.*) Sorry, John! Was that your head under there?

BARNEY. (*Emerging from the kitchen, holding his glass of whisky.*) Jo, is there anything I can do? (Jo *desperately shoves the table out and slams the door on it.*)

Jo. No, thanks, Barney! Just getting the place straight. You go back and make yourself comfortable in the kitchen. (*She tries to urge him along, but he stands his ground. He is now quite noticeably drunk.*)

BARNEY. It's awfully lonely in the kitchen. Jo. I've got no one to talk to out there.

Jo. I'll be out there in a moment. Have another drink.

BARNEY. I've had another drink. I've had several drinks. Ah, Jo! (*He looks round the room sentimentally.*) This room brings back memories! All the times Bee and I have been here, all the happy times we had together . . . This used to be the dinning-room. You used to have a dining-table in here . . . (*He crosses to where the dining-chairs still stand, marking the spot from which the table went. He sits down on one of the chairs, as if he were at the table, while* Jo *shoots anxious glances in*

the direction of the living-room.) You and Stephen . . .
Bee and me . . . Simon and Kay . . . Nicholas and
Jay . . . the glasses gleaming in the candlelight . . .
We used to talk about our children, do you remember?
The little tricks they'd been up to—the funny things
they'd said. And where we'd been on holiday, and what
John and Laura were doing these days. Now it's all over.
Even the table's gone. (Jo *hands him the tray with the
single place setting on it.*)

Jo. There's a perfectly good table in the kitchen,
Barney. Now you take this along with you, and I'll be
out there to give you some soup in half a tick.

BARNEY. (*Taking the tray, and looking at it suspiciously.*) I'm not going to be eating all on my own,
am I?

Jo. No, no, no. That's just to be starting with. I'll
bring the rest of the stuff in a minute.

BARNEY. (*Holding the tray with one hand and putting
the other arm round* Jo.) Don't you leave me, Jo. You're
the only friend I've got left in the whole wide world.
Well, there's Stephen. Where is Stephen? Why's he never
around when anyone wants him? Every time I come in,
he goes out! I don't think Stephen likes me.

Jo. Of course he likes you, Barney. Now, come on, this
way . . .

BARNEY. I probably shouldn't say this, Jo, but you're
wasted on Stephen. Do you know that? I've always
thought so. Time after time I've sat at that table . . .
(*He attempts to return to the site of the table, but she
restrains him.*) . . . and thought, My God, fancy a marvellous girl like Jo being married to a man like Stephen!

Jo. Now, come on, Barney . . .

BARNEY. I mean, old Stephen . . . well, he's a bit of
a stick, isn't he? Not really your type, I should have
thought. Not *my* type, I can tell you that.

Jo. I thought you thought he was just like you?

BARNEY. Do you really thing so? If I'd been around
at the right time you wouldn't have thought that! Old

Stephen wouldn't have stood a chance. I've always been secretly in love with you, Jo. It's not just something I'm saying because Bee's left me . . . Left me for a bloody pouf, did you know that?

Jo. Yes. In here, Barney . . .

BARNEY. (*Suspiciously.*) How do you know that?

Jo. You told me.

BARNEY. Just walked out without a word. Last Wednesday evening. Hair down to here, by all accounts. Well, I ask you, what sort of position does that leave *me* in . . . ? (*She at last manages to push him into the kitchen.*)

Jo. Now you just sit down and relax, and . . . well . . . pour yourself another drink. (*She shuts the door firmly, hurries across to the dining-chairs, and takes the first two to the living-room door. She is just about to open the door when the kitchen door bursts open again, and* BARNEY *comes out.*)

BARNEY. (*Shouting furiously.*) But if I ever get my hands on the little fairy I'll shake him till his wings drop off!

Jo. (*Hurrying across to put him away again.*) Sh! You'll wake the children!

BARNEY. (*Contritely.*) Oh, the children . . . yes . . . Sorry, Jo. Sorry. (*She pushes him back towards the kitchen.*) Let me give you a kiss to show I'm forgiven . . . (BARNEY *kisses Jo clumsily as she bundles him away. She shuts the door, then returns to the chair. She brings the remaining four down to the living-room door. The kitchen door opens again. Jo turns upon it, raises her finger sternly and says 'uh!', as if to make a dog sit down. The door closes again. She opens the living-room door and begins to move the chairs inside.*)

Jo. (*Merrily.*) Chairs! I knew I'd forgotten something . . . ! You're all very quiet in here! Stephen, are you making sure everyone's got plenty to drink? (*As she hands in the last chair,* STEPHEN *emerges, calling back jovially over his shoulder.*)

STEPHEN. David, pour everyone another drink, will you? And do sit down! Bee, you be mother and arrange everyone . . . (*He closes the door, and turns anxiously to* Jo.) What's going on? Where have you been? They're all just getting silently plastered in there, waiting for something to happen.

JO. I've been dealing with Barney. He's just getting noisily plastered in *there*. Thinks he ought to have married me.

STEPHEN. David and Laura shut up like clams at the sight of Alex. Alex hasn't said anything yet, and Bee just keeps looking at him anxiously, as if he might disappear in front of her eyes. For God's sake let's start to eat, before something happens.

JO. I'll get the soup, you get the wine. (*She goes out to the kitchen, he to the living-room.*)

STEPHEN. (*Jovially, as he enters.*) All right?

JO. (*Likewise.*) All right?

STEPHEN. That's right . . .

JO. All right . . . (*They both reappear immediately, he with a bottle of wine which was previously on the table, she with a tureen of soup.*)

STEPHEN. (*To the occupants of the living-room, as he leaves.*) Just got to put some wine in the soup.

JO. (*To* BARNEY, *as she leaves the kitchen.*) Just got to put some soup in the *au pair* . . . (*They cross at speed.*)

STEPHEN. (*Furiously.*) But why does it always happen to *us?*

JO. Stephen, it's going to be *all right!* (STEPHEN *goes into the kitchen, she into the living-room.*)

STEPHEN. (*To* BARNEY, *as he enters.*) Wine that maketh glad the heart of man . . . !

JO. (*To the occupants of the living-room, as she enters.*) Soup! Soup! Beautiful soup! (*They reappear almost at once,* STEPHEN *still holding the bottle of wine,* JO *now holding a single bowl of soup.*)

STEPHEN. (*To* BARNEY, *as he leaves the kitchen.*)

Don't worry—I'll be back. Just got to give the *au pair* a drop.

Jo. (*To the occupants of the living-room, as she leaves.*) Yes, I'll be sitting down in a moment. Just got to drop this in on the *au pair*. (*They cross at speed again.*)

Stephen. By God, you're right! He's as pissed as a newt!

Jo. Some of them are pretty glassy-eyed in there. (*Jo goes into the kitchen*, Stephen *into the living-room.*)

Stephen. (*To the occupants of the living-room, as he enters.*) Wine that maketh glad the heart of man!

Jo. (*To* Barney, *as she enters the kitchen.*) Soup of the evening! Beautiful soup! (*They reappear at once*, Jo *empty-handed*, Stephen *carrying the bread-basket.*)

Stephen. (*To the occupants of the living-room, as he leaves.*) No peace for the wicked!

Jo. (*To* Barney, *as she leaves the kitchen.*) A woman's work is never done! (*They cross at speed.*)

Stephen. (*Desperately.*) They're not saying anything!

Jo. Say something yourself, then! Make conversation! (Jo *goes into the living-room*, Stephen *into the kitchen.*)

Stephen. (*To* Barney, *as he enters.*) You know where Simon and Kay say Nicholas and Jay are going this year . . . ?

Jo. (*To the occupants of the living-room, as she enters.*) Have you heard that story of Nicholas and Jay's about Marcus and Poo . . . ? (*They re-emerge almost at once*, Stephen *still carrying the bottle of wine*, Jo *empty-handed.*)

Stephen. (*To* Barney, *as he leaves.*) . . . and was last seen walking stark naked down Kensington High Street carrying a garden sprinkler and a double bass!

Jo. (*To the occupants of the living-room, as she leaves.*) . . . to which she replied, 'But, Mummy, if you put some toys in your tummy too then he won't *need* to come out'! (*They close their respective doors and lean wearily against them as they catch each other's eyes.*)

STEPHEN. Not a flicker.

JO. Heavens, we've got a slow house in here tonight!

STEPHEN. It's playing these audiences of one out in the sticks the depresses me. How many more courses?

JO. Only three. (*She indicates the living-room.*) You go and sit down in there and talk to them while they have their soup. I'll just get the next course out of the oven, and then I'll join you. (STEPHEN *crosses wearily to the living-room. She kisses him in passing.*) Pour yourself a drink. Just relax and enjoy yourself! (*He gives her a hopeless look. She opens the door for him, and without breaking step he is transformed into the jovial host again.*)

STEPHEN. (*To the occupants of the living-room.*) Did I ever tell you that story of Nicholas and Kay's about Simon and Sue . . . ? (JO *shuts the door behind him and crosses to the kitchen.*)

JO. (*To* BARNEY, *as she enters.*) Shall I tell you where Simon and Kay say Nicholas and Jay are going this year . . . ? (*She backs out again hurriedly.*) *No*, Barney! Now just sit down like a good boy and eat up your soup. I haven't come out here for fun and games. I've just come to fetch the casserole. (*She goes in again, and emerges hurriedly once more, now holding a hot and heavy casserole dish away from her, looking as if she is trying to avoid having her bottom pinched. She turns to face him, and addresses him as if he were one of her children.*) *No*, Barney! No, it's no good looking at me like that, either. I'm not amused. (*She sets down the casserole so that she can close the door.*) Now just you stay here and eat up all your soup and don't come out until I tell you. (*She shuts the door, picks up her casserole, and takes it across to the living-room. She is just opening the door when she realises that the kitchen door has opened again. She closes the living-room door with weary patience.*) Now, Barney, what is it? I thought **I** told you to stay there and finish your dinner.

BARNEY. (*Emerging, and raising his hand.*) Please, Miss, can I be excused?

Jo. (*Sighing impatiently.*) Well, I suppose if you must, you must. (*She nods at the corridor door.*) Through there, turn left, second door on the right.

BARNEY. Thank you, Miss. (*He turns towards the corridor door.*)

Jo. But straight back to the kitchen when you've finished! (*She takes the casserole into the living-room, trying simultaneously to smile at the occupants and to make sternly sure that* BARNEY *is not looking in. As soon as the door shuts* BARNEY *stops, in fuddled indignation.*)

BARNEY. Turn left, second on the right! I've been here once or twice before, you know! I'm an old friend of yours—remember? It's the same story everywhere. They all say how sorry they are, and then they don't want to know you. But this is a new one, I must say, inviting you round and then leaving you to eat on your own in the kitchen, without even the *au pair* girl for company . . . ! It's not catching, you know! My God, when I think of all the dinner-parties Bee and I gave for *them!* All the ghastly evenings I've spent *here*, sitting at the table in this very room . . . ! (*He goes towards where it was, shaking his head.*) Now even the table has gone. (*He stops in his tracks, his lachrymose mood dispelled by astonishment.*) Now even the *chairs* have gone! (*He gazes round in bewilderment.*) What's happening here? They must have . . . They must have taken them out for spring cleaning. Or perhaps . . . they took them out and *sold* them! Well, poor bloody old Stephen and Jo! On their uppers, and never said a word about it! Gave me a bowl of soup when they can't even afford to eat themselves! What a couple of real bricks they are! I must say, you really find out who your friends are when this kind of thing happens. Jo! Stephen! Where are you? (*He goes towards the living-room door.*) There's no need to hide yourselves away! I know what's going on! (*He stops, with his hand on the door handle, as another thought strikes him.*) Oh, I was just going to have a pee, wasn't I . . . (BARNEY *crosses to the corridor door, turning as he goes out to call reassuringly back towards the living-room.*) Don't worry—I'll be right back! What a couple of bricks! (*He goes out. As he does so, the living-room door opens, and* ALEX *enters. He is a beardless young man with a great mop of frizzy hair and bell-bottomed trousers, and is hung about with chains and dingle-dangles; almost completely ambiguous as to sex and class.* JO's *hand shoots out of the living-room door, catches him, and pulls him back.*)

Jo. (*Off.*) Alex! Where are you going?

ALEX. (*Reappearing.*) I'm just looking for, you know, the gents. (*He shuts the door and crosses to the corridor door. Not seeing what he wants out there, he tries the kitchen door. He is just about to open it when the living-room door is flung open, and* STEPHEN *rushes out, still clasping the bottle of wine.*)

STEPHEN. (*Urgently.*) *Alex!* No! (ALEX *abandons the kitchen door as if it had been suddenly electrified, and starts back.* STEPHEN *hurriedly closes the living-room door and runs across to interpose himself bodily between* ALEX *and the kitchen door.*) Not in there, Alex!

ALEX. Oh, sorry. I was just looking for, you know, the kind of, you know . . .

STEPHEN. Well, you won't find it in there!

ALEX. (*Staring at the door curiously in spite of himself.*) Oh, sorry.

STEPHEN. This is the kitchen.

ALEX. Sorry.

STEPHEN. (*Steering him towards the corridor door.*) No, no, no—my fault. I should have shown you where it was in the first place.

ALEX. Well, you know, I didn't want to sort of, you know, put you sort of *out*, like.

STEPHEN. No, no, no—very remiss of me. (*He opens*

the corridor door.) It's just that you looked so much at home here that I'd forgotten you hadn't been to the house before.

ALEX. Oh, well, you know . . .

STEPHEN. But I hope we'll be seeing a lot of you and Bee in the future. In a few mouths time you'll be able to find the way to the john here in your sleep.

ALEX. (*As he is gradually edged through the door.*) Oh, well . . . Yeah, that'd be nice . . .

STEPHEN. Turn left, second on the right. (*He closes the door, hesitates a moment, and then opens it again.*) You'll be all right? Shall I wait for you? I mean, you can find your way back, can you? It's the door immediately opposite, not the one round to the left. That's the kitchen. (STEPHEN *closes the door reluctantly again. He goes to the kitchen door to listen. Apparently reassured, he hurries back to the living-room, resuming his story to the occupants as he enters.*) Yes, so anyway, the upshot of it was the Nicholas had to go to the Ambassador's dressed as a horse . . . ! (*He closes the door behind him. At once* ALEX *reappears from the corridor door.*)

ALEX. It's locked! (*He realises that* STEPHEN *has disappeared.*) Oh . . . (*He looks round the room in despair, and spots a vase of flowers. He crosses to it, looks round the room to make sure no one is coming, then takes the flowers out and retires with the vase behind the window curtains. At once the lavatory flushes off, and* BARNEY *comes back through the corridor door. He goes to the kitchen door, then hesitates.*)

BARNEY. Just a moment. What was I going to do? Oh, find poor old Stephen and Jo. (*He crosses to the living room.*) Come out of there! No need to hide from me!

ALEX. (*Putting his head round the curtain.*) Sorry! I'm just in the middle of something. (BARNEY *stops, and gazes at* ALEX *in astonishment.* ALEX *disappears again.*)

BARNEY. So they have got an au pair girl after all! (*He pulls the curtain back and reveals* ALEX.) Hullo!

ALEX. Oh . . . hi . . .

BARNEY. What's your name, then?

ALEX. Er . . . Alex . . .

BARNEY. Alex. That's a very pretty name.

ALEX. Oh . . . glad you like it . . . (*He moves towards the living-room door.*)

BARNEY. Well, don't rush off, Alex, now you're here. Stay and talk for a bit—I'm all on my own.

ALEX. Oh . . . ! Right . . .

BARNEY. Doesn't it get you down, looking after the children all the time?

ALEX. The kids? No . . . I don't get much trouble. There's the usual business about, you know, pot.

BARNEY. They still use the pot, do they?

ALEX. Oh, yeah, most of them.

BARNEY. That must make a lot of extra work for you.

ALEX. Oh, I just try to stop them getting busted.

BARNEY. The pots?

ALEX. The kids. I mean, you know, I try to sort of keep the fuzz off their necks as much as possible.

BARNEY. That's a problem, is it, the fuzz on their necks?

ALEX. Oh, you get the fuzz round, you know, twice a night, sometimes.

BARNEY. It's funny, Alex—I feel I can talk to you. I feel we somehow understand each other. Do you feel that?

ALEX. (*Politely.*) Oh . . . well . . . you know . . .

BARNEY. (*Putting his arm around* ALEX.) I mean, I expect I seem rather old to you, don't I?

ALEX. No, no . . .

BARNEY. You're probably thinking, who is this terrible dirty old man, coming and putting his arm round me like this?

ALEX. No, I mean, you've got to be, you know, sort of open-minded about this kind of thing, haven't you?

BARNEY. I expect you're wondering if I'm married.

ALEX. No, honestly, I'm not wondering anything . . .

BARNEY. Well, I wouldn't tell this to anyone else, Alex, but she's walked out on me. My wife. Without so much as a by-your-leave. One moment she was there, and the next—woof!—she was gone. But do you know who she's gone off with? She's gone off with a pouf! What do you think of that?

ALEX. (*Obviously unable to decide what he is supposed to think of this.*) Oh . . . well . . .

BARNEY. I mean, she used to try and tell me I was a bit obsessional. But she!— She's a complete raving neurotic! You ought to meet her, Alex!

ALEX. Yes, well, there's this bird I'm, you know, going around with at the moment . . .

BARNEY. You . . . go around with birds, too, do you, Alex?

ALEX. Yeah . . . I mean, birds are more, you know, my thing. I mean, no offence . . .

BARNEY. No, I admire you for it, Alex! It's this tremendous broad-mindedness, this wonderful openness to experience that my generation lacks. I mean, take my wife. She's just a mass of repressions and inhibitions— that's why she's so neurotic.

ALEX. Yes, well, this bird's like that. This bird I'm, you know, going round with. Thinks everyone's getting at her all the time.

BARNEY. My wife—exactly the same!

ALEX. Oh, they're all the same, in my opinion.

BARNEY. I mean, we'd go out to dinner somewhere, and I'd put my arm round some girl I'd known for donkey's years—just like I'm doing now, just the same, nothing more in it than that—and I'd look round, and my wife would have disappeared. And do you know where she'd be?

ALEX. In the bathroom, crying her eyes out.

BARNEY. (*Agreeing, wonderingly.*) In the bathroom, crying her eyes out!

ALEX. I mean, so *jealous* . . . !

BARNEY. My God, it's marvellous meeting someone who *understands* like this!

ALEX. It's fantastic being able to, you know, sort of

get it off your chest, at last, isn't it? I mean, this bird I'm talking about . . .

BARNEY. (*Interrupting.*) Would you like a drink, Alex? I've got a drop of Scotch out here. Yes, go on . . . (*He goes into the kitchen. ALEX follows him as far as the door, and stands talking there as a hand first holds up the bottle of whisky, then a moment later proffers a full glass.*)

ALEX. I mean, I can see why she's so, you know, hung up. She's married to this bloke who's even nuttier than she is . . . Thanks . . . They'd go out to a party, or something, and the first thing she knew she'd find him out in the kitchen, feeling up the bird who was giving the party and telling her that it was her he'd really meant to marry all the time. Well, it would make anyone insecure, wouldn't it? And you know what he did once . . . ? (*The hand reappears holding a second glass of whisky, clinks it against his, and disappears. ALEX raises his glass.*) The same to you. (*He drinks down the whisky.*) He got so, you know, stoned, he went out to the kitchen started feeling up the bird's husband by mistake, and telling *him* the tale! (*The arm appears and ushers him into the kitchen. The door closes. At once the living-room door opens and STEPHEN comes out, still holding the bottle of wine, and addressing the occupants.*)

STEPHEN. . . . but above all, surely, it's a question of setting the present economic crisis within the context of European cultural structure . . . (*He closes the door, and looks anxiously round the room, calling in a stage whisper.*) Alex . . . ? Alex . . . ! (*He crosses to the corridor door, and calls off.*) Alex! Are you all right! (*There being no answer, he goes out to investigate, and returns an instant later, baffled. He notices that the curtain is disarranged, crosses to it, and finds the vase behind. Frowning, he replaces the flowers. As he does so, the kitchen door opens, and the broken remains of the dicky dining chair are thrown out. He spins round, and picks the chair up.*) Barney! What have you done with this chair? (*He tries to open the kitchen door, but it is locked.*) Barney! Barney . . . ? What's happening? Why won't this door open? Why have you locked the door, Barney? And what have you been doing to this chair! All right, the leg was loose—but to get it into this condition you'd have needed two people sitting on it or something . . . ! (*The implication of his words strikes him. He turns back to the door.*) Barney . . . ! *Barney* . . . ! (*The living-room door opens, and* BEE *enters. She is wearing some astonishing minimal see-through type of outfit, more suitable to someone ten years younger.*)

BEE. (*Anxiously.*) Stephen . . .

STEPHEN. (*Whirling round, and attempting to hide the very existence of the kitchen door.*) Bee!

BEE. Where's Alex?

STEPHEN. I'm not quite sure, Bee. Around somewhere.

BEE. Perhaps he's in the kitchen . . .

STEPHEN. (*Guarding it.*) No, no, no—I've looked. There's no one there. He went to the loo, originally.

BEE. He can't still be in the loo, can he?

STEPHEN. (*Urging her.*) Why don't you just go and look?

BEE. I mean, I don't want to fuss. He can't stand me fussing.

STEPHEN. But all the same . . .

BEE. All the same, if something had happened to him . . .

STEPHEN. (*Holding the corridor door open for her.*) First on the left, second on the right.

BEE. Oh, I expect he just got bored and went home.

STEPHEN. (*Seizing on this explanation with relief.*) Yes, he did!

BEE. (*Surprised.*) He did?

STEPHEN. Of course he did! I forgot to tell you. He said he had a headache, so he was going home. He just slipped quietly out the back so as not to break up the party. How stupid of me to forget! (BEE *gazes at him for a moment, and then suddenly gives a loud despairing wail and bursts into tears.*) What? What is it, Bee? What's the matter? (*He puts a baffled protecting arm around her, looking back anxiously over his shoulder at the kitchen. She seizes him gratefully and cries into his chest.*) Sh, Bee! What is it?

BEE. Don't you see? He's left me!

STEPHEN. Left you?

BEE. I *knew* he would! I *knew* it couldn't last!

STEPHEN. He hasn't left you, Bee! He's just gone home with a headache!

BEE. Headache!

STEPHEN. He said he'd ring you tomorrow. (*But this makes* BEE *give a cry of fresh pain, and weep more bitterly still.*) No, he said he'd ring you *tonight* . . . (*But this makes it worse still.*) He's going to ring you the moment you get in! So you see he hasn't left you, has he, Bee!

BEE. (*Bitterly.*) He wouldn't have to ring me if he hadn't moved out, would he? (*She wails more loudly than ever.*)

STEPHEN. No, well, I've got that wrong. (*He looks round anxiously at the kitchen door.*) I didn't mean he was going to *ring* you, exactly. I meant . . .

BEE. Oh, shut up, Stephen! You're just making it worse!

STEPHEN. No, what I meant was . . .

BEE. Oh, Stephen! You're the only friend I've got left in the world! Don't you leave me!

STEPHEN. No, I won't, but . . .

BEE. Alex has walked out on me. Barney hates me. All my friends have turned against me because of Alex. All Alex's friends treat me as if I were his mother. Jo's afraid I'll have an affair with you next . . . You're the only person left, Stephen! I've always felt you were the one man I could really talk to. If only we'd met earlier it could all have been so simple! (*She embraces him hysterically. He looks wildly from door to door, uncertain as to which he would less welcome intervention from.*)

STEPHEN. Sh! Sh! Calm down now!

BEE. Oh, Stephen!

STEPHEN. (*Disengaging himself with difficulty.*) Now, you just wait here . . . and I'll go and fetch you a nice stiff calming drink . . .

BEE. (*Seizing him again.*) Don't leave me!

STEPHEN. I shan't be a minute . . . You just sit down and relax . . . (*He attempts to set the broken chair for her, then realises what he is doing and picks it up again.*) I mean, you just stand up and relax . . . (*He goes out through the living-room door, resuming his conversation with the occupants as he does so.*) . . . and, of course, of setting European cultural structure within the context of our repressed sexual fantasies . . . (*He disappears and shuts the door. At the sight of the door shutting BEE gives way to a new burst of despair.*)

BEE. Now they've all gone! They've all left me! I've no one to turn to! (*She in fact turns towards the kitchen door, and leans against it in melodramatic despair, in the attitude of Love Locked Out.*) No one! No one! (*Suddenly she stops crying and lifts her hand from the door. She listens, frowning, then puts her ear to the door and listens again, puzzled.*) Alex! That's Alex's voice! (*BEE turns away from the door, opens her handbag, and hastily begins to refurbish her appearance.*) Oh God! Mustn't let him see I was worried . . . Cheerful smile, knew he was there all the time . . . (*As she finishes this task the door opens, and BARNEY comes thoughtfully out. She closes her bag and turns to him, smiling.*) Alex!

BARNEY. (*Putting his arm round her confidentially.*) Jo, there's something I think you ought to know about that *au pair* girl of yours . . . (*His voice dies away as he gets his gaze properly focused on her. She is staring at him, transfixed with astonishment.*) Bee!

BEE. Barney! (*For a moment they just stare at each other, still embraced. Then, abruptly, BEE breaks away and opens the kitchen door to see who is inside. Hastily BARNEY pulls it shut again.*)

BARNEY. Friend of mine, that's all.

BEE. You and Alex . . . ?

BARNEY. We were just having a friendly conversation
—nothing more to it.

BEE. (*Wildly.*) You and Alex—having a friendly conversation? It's a conspiracy! Getting together behind my
back! (*She turns and rushes off, weeping, through the
corridor door.*)

BARNEY. (*Following her as far as the door.*) No, Bee,
listen . . . ! Stop . . . ! (*He is going to pursue her
further, but at that moment the kitchen door opens. He
runs back to it.*) Now you keep out of this! You've caused
enough trouble already! (*He puts his hand round the
door and takes the key out of the lock on the other side.*)
Au pair girl! My God, I knew young people were confused, but I didn't know the rot had gone this far! (*He
slams the door shut and locks it. Then, pocketing the
key, he runs back to the corridor door.*) Bee! Listen! Let
me explain . . . ! (*He seizes the handle of the corridor
door and pushes, assuming in his anxiety that it opens
the same way as the kitchen door. But it doesn't. He
calls imperiously.*) Open the door! Come on, open the
door! *Open this door!* (*He hammers on it, then suddenly
drops his commanding manner, and becomes pleading instead.*) Look, Bee, it's all a misunderstanding! You
looked in there, you thought it was the *au pair* girl,
didn't you? *I* thought it was the *au pair* girl! But listen,
Bee, you open this door and I'll tell you an astonishing
fact . . . Bee . . . ! (*He turns away from the door for
a moment, amazed at himself.*) Though why the hell *I*
should be excusing myself to *her* . . . ! (*He addresses
himself furiously to the door again, hammering and
shouting.*) Open this door at once! I know what you're
doing—you needn't think I don't! You're in the bathroom, having a good old weep!

GIRL CHILD'S VOICE. (*Calling, from off.*) Mummy!
Mummy! There's a lady crying in the bathroom!

BARNEY. (*Shouting at the top of his voice.*) Look, *stop*

crying in the bathroom, and come down and open this door! (*He rains a frustrated fusillade of blows upon the door, then stops, realising that someone else somewhere is hammering on a door. He runs furiously across to the kitchen, and shouts through the closed door.*) Stop that noise at once! I can scarcely hear myself knock! (*There is another salvo of bangs from the kitchen, to which he bangs furiously back.*) One more bang out of you, my girl, and I'll put the police on to you, my lad! (*He runs furiously back to the corridor door and thunders on that one again.*) Come downstairs this instant and open the door! (BARNEY *shouts and thunders.* ALEX *thunders, too. There is a sudden brief lull, during which the living-room door opens, and* Jo *enters, holding a nice stiff calming drink, and talking back over her shoulder to the occupants of the living-room.*)

Jo. . . . in which case, so much for European cultural structure . . . ! (*She closes the door.*)

BARNEY. (*To* Jo, *in furious explanation.*) She's in the bathroom, weeping!

Jo. Stephen said she needed a stiff drink . . .

BARNEY. She'll need more than a stiff drink if I ever get my hands on her! (*He whirls back upon the door, pounding on it and shouting at the top of his voice.*) Can't you understand? I'm trying to tell you I love you!

Jo. Why don't you go up and tell her at slightly closer range?

BARNEY. Because the little bitch has locked the door! (*He hurls his weight against it to demonstrate.*)

Jo. It opens this way.

BARNEY. (*Almost too furious to comprehend.*) What?

Jo. Pull it. (*He pulls it violently. It opens without let or hindrance, sending him reeling back into the room. As he picks himself up there is another salvo of knocking from the kitchen.*) What's that?

BARNEY. That's your friend Alex. I've locked him in the kitchen pending his arrest on a variety of serious charges . . . All *right!* I'm coming . . . ! (*He rushes out through the corridor door. There is the noise of heavy feet thundering up the stairs, then of rending wood, and then of glass objects smashing. Calmly,* Jo *goes over to the corridor door.*)

BOY CHILD'S VOICE. (*Calling, from off.*) Mummy! *Mummy!* There's a lady and a man fighting in the bathroom!

Jo. Go to *sleep,* dear! I don't want to hear another sound out of you two—you know we've got people to dinner. (*With philosophical calm* Jo *closes the door, to deaden the continuing noise. There is another salvo of blows from the kitchen. She raises her eyebrows wearily, notices the nice stiff calming drink still in her hand, and drinks it down stoically. As she finishes it, the living-room door opens, and* STEPHEN *creeps quietly out, looking anxiously back over his shoulder and smiling benignly. He shuts the door behind him.* Jo *reports the situation to him with calm detachment.*) Barney and Bee are fighting in the bathroom. Alex and the rest of dinner are locked in the kitchen. The children are awake.

STEPHEN. David and Dora are asleep.

Jo. John and Laura. Are you sure?

STEPHEN. They hadn't said anything for quite a while. I don't know whether you'd noticed. (Jo *opens the living-room door. She and* STEPHEN *both gaze off at* JOHN *and* LAURA. *Bursts of noise from bathroom and kitchen continue intermittently.*) It was the economic crisis that finished them, I think.

Jo. I knew we should have kept off politics.

STEPHEN. They look quite peaceful.

Jo. I *think* they quite enjoyed the evening, didn't they?

STEPHEN. Oh, I think everyone did, all things considered.

Jo. I think it all went off reasonably well.

STEPHEN. Jo, I'm sorry I shouted at you earlier.

Jo. I lost my temper, too. It always gets a bit tense when people are coming to dinner. You always think everything's going to go wrong.

STEPHEN. It seems so ridiculous afterwards. You can't think what you were so worried about. *(Somewhere a window is smashed.)*

JO. *(With relief.)* Anyway, that's four people we owed dinner to knocked off.

STEPHEN. Five!

JO. Yes! The only trouble is, we haven't had anything to eat ourselves. I'm starving.

STEPHEN. So am I. Let's run around the corner and have a plate of fish and chips. *(They creep out through the living room.)*

CURTAIN

Also By
Michael Frayn

ALARMS AND EXCURSIONS

ALPHABETICAL ORDER

AUDIENCE

BALMORAL

BENEFACTORS

CLOUDS

COPENHAGEN

DEMOCRACY

DONKEYS' YEARS

EXCHANGE

HERE

LISTEN TO THIS

MAKE AND BREAK

NOISES OFF

NOW YOU KNOW

WILD HONEY

Lightning Source UK Ltd.
Milton Keynes UK
UKOW031504270613

212840UK00001B/5/P